TARUN TAKSHAY

Decode YouTube Algorithm

TAKSHAY
DIGITAL ACADEMY

First published by Takshay Digital Academy 2025

First edition

ISBN: 978-93-344-4989-1

This book was professionally typeset on Reedsy.
Find out more at reedsy.com

Contents

1

The Evolution of YouTube

"The future belongs to those who adapt."

"YouTube isn't just a video platform anymore—it's the second biggest search engine in the world, and the biggest stage where anyone can perform."

My Personal Experience

When I first stepped into YouTube, I thought it was just about uploading videos and waiting for views to come. I believed that if my video was "good," people would automatically find it and it would go viral. I used to spend nights editing, sometimes re-recording the same clip ten times, hoping this one video would change my life.

But days turned into weeks, and weeks into months. My videos barely touched 100 views. I would check analytics every morning with so much hope, only to see the same flat graph staring back at me. At one point, I even thought maybe YouTube was "broken" or it was biased toward big creators.

It was only later, after researching and experimenting, that I realized one simple truth: **YouTube is always changing, and those who adapt to these changes win the game.**

This is why before we jump into algorithms, thumbnails, and growth hacks, we must first understand how YouTube itself has *evolved.*

The Birth of YouTube (2005–2006)

- YouTube started in 2005 as a simple platform where people could upload short clips.
- Fun fact: The first-ever video was "Me at the Zoo," uploaded by co-founder Jawed Karim.
- Back then, it was mostly random home videos, pranks, and funny clips. No one imagined it would turn into a billion-dollar industry.

Lesson: In the beginning, YouTube wasn't about money or fame—it was about expression. And even today, the best channels are built on *authentic expression first, strategy second.*

Google's Acquisition (2006–2010)

- In 2006, Google bought YouTube for $1.65 billion. That's when things got serious.
- Google added search engine power, ads, and started refining recommendations.
- Creators could now **monetize videos through Adsense** (2007). This is when people realized: *"Wait... I can actually make a career out of this!"*

Lesson: YouTube shifted from a hobby platform to a business platform.

The Rise of Professional Creators (2010–2015)

- Channels like PewDiePie, Smosh, and Jenna Marbles grew into global icons.
- YouTube launched **the Partner Program** allowing creators to earn consistently.
- Smartphones exploded → suddenly everyone had a camera in their pocket.
- YouTube also introduced **HD videos, live streaming, and better analytics**.

Lesson: Quality and consistency started becoming important. The casual hobbyist was now competing with semi-professional creators.

YouTube Becomes a Career (2015–2020)

- Watch time became the #1 ranking factor.
- The algorithm shifted focus: instead of just clicks, it started rewarding **how long viewers stayed**.
- Features like Community Tab, Super Chat, Memberships gave creators new income streams.
- This was also the rise of *niche channels*: cooking, fitness, education, gaming, reviews.

Lesson: YouTube became more than "viral videos." It became an ecosystem of learning, entertainment, and careers.

The Modern YouTube (2020–Now)

- YouTube Shorts was introduced to compete with TikTok.
- AI recommendations became sharper: the algorithm now knows what you'll watch before *you* do.
- Creators started diversifying: ads + sponsors + digital products + courses.
- The competition is higher, but so are the opportunities.

Lesson: Today, YouTube is like a university + marketplace + entertainment hub—all in one. If you adapt, you win. If you stay stuck in 2015 strategies, you lose.

Why Most Creators Fail

- They don't study the platform. They keep using outdated methods.
- They upload random content without a clear niche.
- They treat YouTube as a lottery, not as a skill-based game.

Truth: Success on YouTube isn't about luck—it's about strategy, persistence, and adapting with the platform's changes.

Action Steps for Readers

1. Write down what year you started watching or uploading on YouTube.
2. Compare how the platform looked then vs now.
3. Ask yourself: *Am I creating content for the YouTube of today, or the YouTube of the past?*

2

The Algorithm Demystified

"If you know the rules of the game, winning gets easier."

"The algorithm isn't your enemy—it's your biggest partner if you learn how it thinks."

My Personal Experience

When I first heard about "the algorithm," it felt like a mystery monster. People would say, *"The algorithm hates me"* or *"YouTube doesn't push my videos."* I used to believe the same. After uploading multiple videos that barely got traction, I convinced myself that the algorithm was against small creators like me.

But one day, I stumbled upon a surprising realization. The algorithm wasn't ignoring me—it was simply following a set of rules. It didn't care who I was, how many subscribers I had, or how much effort I put into editing. It only cared about one thing: **whether viewers liked my video enough to keep watching.**

That day changed everything. Once I stopped blaming the algorithm and started learning how it really works, my results improved. Suddenly, I could see why some videos performed and others didn't. It felt like I had finally discovered the hidden map of YouTube.

The Truth About the Algorithm

YouTube's algorithm is not a person. It has no feelings, no bias, and no personal agenda. It is a machine—an advanced system built by Google to achieve one single goal: **keep viewers on YouTube for as long as possible.**

If your video helps YouTube achieve that goal, the algorithm will reward you by showing your content to more people. If it doesn't, your video gets buried. It's that simple.

The Core Metrics YouTube Cares About

Click-Through Rate (CTR)

- CTR is the percentage of people who clicked on your video after seeing it.
- If 100 people see your thumbnail and 10 click, that's a 10% CTR.
- A higher CTR tells YouTube, "People are interested in this video."

Watch Time

- Watch time is the total number of minutes viewers spend watching your video.
- A 2-minute video with high clicks but low watch time will lose to a 10-minute video that holds attention.

Audience Retention

- Retention measures what percentage of your video people watch.
- If most viewers leave after 30 seconds, the algorithm will stop recommending it.
- If viewers stay until the end, the algorithm boosts it.

Engagement (Likes, Comments, Shares, Subscribes)

- Engagement signals to YouTube that your content is meaningful.
- But remember: engagement is secondary. Retention and watch time still matter more.

Myths vs. Truths

- **Myth 1:** Tags are the most important factor.
- **Truth:** Tags have minimal impact today. Titles, descriptions, and thumbnails matter more.
- **Myth 2:** Uploading daily guarantees growth.
- **Truth:** Quality + retention beats quantity. Consistency helps, but bad content uploaded daily won't perform.
- **Myth 3:** You need millions of subscribers to get recommended.
- **Truth:** YouTube recommends videos, not channels. A brand-new creator can go viral with one good video.

The Algorithm as a Shopkeeper

Think of YouTube like a giant shopping mall. The algorithm is the shopkeeper, and videos are the products. The shopkeeper's job is to offer the customer (viewer) the best product that will keep them inside the mall longer.

If your product (video) is attractive, engaging, and satisfies the customer's interest, the shopkeeper will keep recommending it to more people. If not, it gets pushed to the back shelf.

A Turning Point in My Journey

When I finally looked at my analytics and noticed my videos had a strong CTR but weak retention, I understood why they weren't taking off. People clicked my thumbnails but left quickly because the introduction was too long and boring.

So, I changed my approach. I started focusing on strong hooks in the first 10 seconds. The result? My retention graph improved, and within weeks, YouTube started recommending my videos more often. It wasn't magic—it was simply aligning with what the algorithm wanted.

Action Steps for You

1. Open your YouTube Studio analytics. Look at CTR, watch time, and audience retention for your last five videos.
2. Identify which metric is weakest. Is it low CTR? Poor retention? Weak watch time?
3. Write down one improvement you will make in your next video to address that weakness.

Closing Thoughts

The algorithm isn't an enemy standing in your way. It is a mirror reflecting how viewers respond to your videos. If you learn to satisfy your viewers, the algorithm will become your best partner.

3

Content That Wins

"Don't just chase views, chase impact."

"The right content can make the algorithm your best friend."

My Personal Experience

When I first started, I made the mistake of uploading all kinds of random videos—tech reviews, motivational talks, tutorials, even vlogs about my daily life. I thought more variety meant more chances of success. But the reality was the opposite.

Some videos got a few views, others barely got noticed, and my channel had no identity. Viewers who came for one video didn't care about the next one because it was about a completely different topic. I was confused, and my subscribers were confused too.

The breakthrough came when I narrowed down to a **niche**. Instead of trying to please everyone, I focused on one audience and one problem I could solve consistently. That shift changed everything. My content started to align, my viewers knew what to expect, and the algorithm finally began recommending my videos more widely.

Why Content Is the Foundation

The algorithm may decide *who sees your video*, but it's your content that decides whether they *stay and subscribe.* No amount of SEO tricks or flashy thumbnails will save a video if the content itself doesn't connect with the audience.

Think of content as the **engine** of your channel. The algorithm is just the fuel. Without a strong engine, no amount of fuel will move you forward.

Evergreen vs. Trending Content

Evergreen Content

- Timeless topics that people will search for year after year.
- Example: "How to Lose Weight at Home," "How to Start a YouTube Channel."
- Pros: Long-term growth, steady traffic.
- Cons: Slower initial traction.

Trending Content

- Topics based on current events, viral trends, or breaking news.
- Example: "YouTube Shorts Update 2025," "New iPhone Review."
- Pros: Quick spikes in views, chance to go viral.
- Cons: Traffic dies down once the trend fades.

Best Strategy: Balance both. Use trending content for quick boosts, but build your foundation on evergreen topics that keep working for you even years later.

Finding Your Niche

Your niche is the intersection of three things:

1. **Passion** – What topics excite you enough to create regularly?
2. **Skill** – What knowledge or expertise do you have that others don't?
3. **Demand** – What are people actually searching for on YouTube?

When you find the overlap, you've found your sweet spot.
Example:

- Passion: Fitness
- Skill: Home workouts without equipment
- Demand: Millions searching for "workout at home"

→ Resulting Niche: "Home Fitness for Beginners"

The Algorithm Loves Consistency of Content

One big mistake creators make is uploading completely unrelated videos. Imagine subscribing to a cooking channel, but the next upload is about car reviews. You'd unsubscribe immediately.

The algorithm reacts the same way. It thrives on patterns. If you repeatedly create content in one niche, YouTube learns who your audience is and recommends your videos to the right people.

Case Study: The Power of Focus

Channel A uploads random videos: one on gaming, one on travel, one on tech. Each video struggles because the audience is scattered.

Channel B focuses on just "Budget Travel Tips." Every video builds on the last, attracting the same type of audience. Within months, the channel grows steadily.

Lesson: Don't confuse the algorithm—and don't confuse your audience. Pick a lane and drive in it.

Action Steps for Readers

1. Write down three topics you are passionate about.
2. List three skills or areas of expertise you already have.
3. Research what people are searching for in those areas using YouTube search suggestions or tools like TubeBuddy and VidIQ.
4. Circle the overlap. That's your niche.
5. Plan your next five videos around that niche.

Closing Thoughts

Content is not about luck—it's about clarity and consistency. If your videos solve a specific problem or fulfill a clear desire for viewers, the algorithm will reward you by connecting you with more of the same audience.

4

Titles, Thumbnails & CTR

"Your video doesn't fail because of content. It fails because nobody clicks."

"The click is the first battle; the video is the second."

My Personal Experience

I once uploaded what I believed was my best tutorial—clear steps, great pacing, strong value. It got almost no views. I felt defeated. A week later, I changed only two things: the title and the thumbnail. Within 24 hours the video woke up. Impressions turned into clicks, and the same content started getting recommended. That day I learned a painful truth: YouTube can't judge your video if no one clicks. The recommendation system promotes what people choose to watch, not what creators hope they'll watch.

Since then, I've treated titles and thumbnails as a craft. When a video under-performs, I don't complain—I test a sharper title and a clearer thumbnail. More often than not, CTR rises and the video breathes again.

Why CTR Rules the First 24–72 Hours

- **CTR (Click-Through Rate)** = people who clicked ÷ people who saw the impression.
- A strong CTR tells YouTube: "Viewers are choosing this."
- **CTR + Watch Time** together signal "quality + relevance." You need both.
- If CTR is weak, YouTube reduces testing. If CTR improves, testing expands.

Practical benchmark (guidance, not a rule):

- Browse/Recommended: 4–10% can be healthy depending on niche and reach.
- Search: 2–6% is common because impressions are broader and more competitive.
- Very broad audiences usually mean lower CTR; niche audiences can achieve higher CTR.

The Winning Pair: Title-Thumbnail Interlock

Think of the title and thumbnail as a team:

- **Thumbnail = concept** (the "what").
- **Title = context** (the "why now").
- If both say the same thing, it's repetitive and dull. If they complement each other, curiosity rises.

Example

- Niche: YouTube growth
- Thumbnail text: "0 to 1,000 Subs" (big, bold, simple)
- Title: "The 90-Day Plan You've Never Tried (Works in Any Niche)"

They're not repeating; they're completing.

Title Craft: Formulas That Consistently Work

Use these as starting points, then customize for your niche and video promise.

How-To + Specific Outcome + Time/Constraint

- "How I Got 1,000 Subs in 30 Days (Without Uploading Daily)"

Mistakes/Traps + Audience

- "7 Thumbnail Mistakes Killing Your CTR"

Numbered Blueprint

- "The 3-Video Growth System: What to Post on Monday, Wednesday, Friday"

Secret/Behind-the-Scenes (Only use when you truly deliver)

- "What Actually Triggers YouTube Recommendations Now"

Versus/Choice

- "Shorts vs Long-Form: Which Grows Faster in 2025?"

Before/After Transformation

- "I Fixed This Title and CTR Jumped 78% (Full Breakdown)"

Challenge/Experiment

- "I Rewrote 10 Titles in 10 Minutes—Here's What Happened"

Myth/Reality

- "Tags Don't Rank Videos. Here's What Does."

For/Against

- "Stop Posting Daily. Do This Instead."

Template/Toolkit

- "Steal My 12 High-CTR Title Templates (Free Swipe File)"

Title rules that protect CTR

- Put the **strongest word first** or second.
- **Shorter often wins** (55–70 characters is a useful ceiling).
- **Clarity beats cleverness.** If they need to think, they won't click.
- **Avoid clickbait** you can't fulfill. You'll kill retention and trust.

Thumbnail Craft: Ten Rules That Win Clicks

1. **One idea only.** If a stranger can't explain it in one sentence, it's too busy.
2. **Big subject, clean background.** Faces or key objects should be large.
3. **Text: 0–4 words max.** The thumbnail is not a poster.
4. **Contrast.** Foreground pops; background recedes.
5. **Directional focus.** Eyes, arrows, circles guide attention to the key element.
6. **Readable at 2 inches.** Zoom out to 10% when designing—still legible?
7. **Emotion.** Neutral faces underperform; show tension, surprise, relief,

pride—whatever fits the story.

8. **Brand, lightly.** Consistent style helps recognition; don't let branding overpower the concept.
9. **No tiny logos or clutter.** If it doesn't help the click, remove it.
10. **Truth in advertising.** Align the promise with the content to protect retention.

Bad vs Good (text-only description)

- Bad: tiny subject, five different phrases, busy background, dull colors.
- Good: close-up face with a strong expression, two words "1k Subs," bright background, one prop (YouTube icon) pointing to the concept.

The 5-Second Title Test

Before you publish, read your title aloud and answer:

1. What's the **promise**?
2. Why **now**?
3. Who is this **for**?
4. What makes it **different** from similar videos?
5. Can I **deliver** the promise in the first 30–60 seconds?

If any answer is weak, iterate.

CTR Repair: When a Good Video Isn't Clicking

Your content might be strong but under-watched. Fix the front door.

1. **Scan Impressions vs Views.** If impressions are high but views are low, CTR is the issue.
2. **Rewrite the Title** in three versions: "Direct," "Curiosity," and "Outcome."

3. **Redesign the Thumbnail** around one clear concept. Remove 50% of elements.
4. **Refresh Update.** Change title and thumbnail together; annotate your change date.
5. **Monitor 48–72 Hours.** If CTR rises and retention holds, keep it. If not, test the second option.

Search vs Browse: Title Nuances

- **Search-focused videos** benefit from straightforward keyword-led titles:
- "How to Edit YouTube Shorts in CapCut (Step-by-Step)"
- **Browse/Recommended** videos often win with curiosity + outcome:
- "I Edited 30 Shorts in 1 Day—Here's What I Learned"

Hybrid approach: Front-load a keyword for relevance, end with a sharp promise for curiosity.

Shorts Thumbnails and Titles

- Shorts may show auto-generated frames; your **first second** acts like a "moving thumbnail."
- Open with a **visual hook** that communicates the idea instantly.
- Titles still matter for searchability and context, even if the viewer sees them later.

Real-World Swipe File (Customize These)

- "You're Editing Wrong: The First 10 Seconds Decide Everything"
- "This Thumbnail Framework Tripled My CTR (Examples Inside)"
- "I Copied MrBeast's Hook Structure—Did It Work?"
- "Zero to 1000 Subscribers: The 90-Day Upload Plan"
- "Stop Using These 5 Words in Titles (Data-Backed)"
- "I Changed Only the Title. Watch What Happened."

- "Beginner to Pro Thumbnails: The 7-Point Checklist"
- "Your Videos Don't Suck. Your Packaging Does."
- "Browse vs Search: Why Your CTR Is Lying to You"
- "From 3% to 9% CTR: My Exact Rewrite Process"

The Packaging Workflow I Use

1. **Define the core promise** before scripting. If you can't state it in one sentence, the video is vague.
2. **Draft 10 title options** fast. Don't self-censor.
3. **Pick 2–3 finalists** and craft thumbnails to match each.
4. **Ask two questions:**

- Which pairing makes me want to click—instantly?
- Does the thumbnail add something the title doesn't?

Ship, then watch early data: CTR, average view duration, and first 30-second retention.

Iterate within the first 72 hours if needed.

Data-Driven Iteration

- **Low CTR + High Retention** → Repackage (new title/thumbnail).
- **High CTR + Low Retention** → Your packaging over-promised or your hook is weak. Fix the intro and pacing.
- **Low CTR + Low Retention** → Topic–audience mismatch. Reassess the angle.

Pre-Upload CTR Checklist (10 Points)

1. One clear idea the audience cares about.
2. Title communicates outcome or tension.
3. Thumbnail communicates concept visually (not repeating title).
4. 0–4 words on thumbnail; readable at a glance.
5. High contrast; subject is large.
6. No clutter, no tiny logos.
7. Promise is deliverable in the first minute.
8. Title under ~70 characters.
9. Three alternative titles explored.
10. Thumbnail tested at small size and against competing thumbnails in your niche.

Action Steps

1. Take your last three underperforming videos.
2. For each, write three new titles and design two new thumbnails.
3. Pick the best pairing and update one video today.
4. Track CTR, impressions, and views for 72 hours after the change.
5. Document what improved. Build your personal packaging rules from results.

Closing Thoughts

Titles and thumbnails are not decoration; they are the front door to your content. When you honor the viewer's time and attention with clear, compelling packaging—and then deliver on that promise—you earn the click and the watch. Do this repeatedly and the algorithm will meet you halfway.

5

Watch Time & Retention

"The first 30 seconds decide your success."

"The algorithm only loves videos that people love to finish."

My Personal Experience

Early in my journey, I had a video that started strong. The CTR was great—people were clicking my thumbnail. But when I checked analytics, the retention graph looked like a cliff. Viewers left within the first 20 seconds. That video never grew, no matter how good the content was after the introduction.

On the other hand, I had another video where I opened with a bold question and delivered value immediately. That retention curve stayed strong, and the algorithm pushed the video far beyond my subscriber base.

That's when I realized: **getting the click is half the battle, keeping attention is the real war.**

Why Retention Matters

Watch time and audience retention are the most important signals YouTube uses to decide if your video deserves wider reach.

- **Watch Time** = total minutes viewers spend watching.
- **Retention** = percentage of the video viewers complete.

YouTube promotes videos that maximize both because they keep people on the platform.

The First 30 Seconds Rule

Most viewers decide whether to stay or leave within the first half-minute.
Mistakes that kill early retention:

- Long, drawn-out intros.
- Repeating your title in the video unnecessarily.
- Telling viewers what you'll do instead of just doing it.

Fix: Start with impact. Ask a big question, make a bold promise, or show the outcome upfront.

Hooks That Work

Start with the Result

- Show what they'll achieve, then explain how.
- Example: "Here's the thumbnail that tripled my CTR. Now let me show you why it worked."

Open a Loop

- Tease information but don't resolve it immediately.
- Example: "I'll reveal the single change that saved my channel—but first, let's understand why most videos fail."

Surprise or Contradiction

- Challenge assumptions.
- Example: "You don't need to upload daily to grow. In fact, it might be killing your channel."

Ask a Powerful Question

- "Why do some videos with average quality get millions of views while better videos flop?"

Pacing and Flow

Retention is not just about the start. It's about **keeping energy steady**.

- **Cut the fluff.** Every sentence should earn its place.
- **Change the scene or visual every 20–30 seconds.** Even small changes help.
- **Summarize and reset.** Remind viewers where they are in the journey.
- **Build tension.** Use mini-cliffhangers: "But here's where most creators go wrong..."

The Retention Graph: How to Read and Fix

Inside YouTube Studio, the retention graph is a goldmine.

- **Sharp drop at the start:** Weak hook or long intro.
- **Gradual decline:** Natural, but can be improved with pacing.
- **Spikes:** Viewers re-watched that part—replicate this style.

- **Flat spots:** Audience is fully engaged. Study why it worked.

My Turning Point

When I started analyzing my retention graphs honestly, I realized most of my viewers were leaving because of one thing: I was taking too long to get to the point. The moment I began cutting introductions, showing value in the first 15 seconds, and editing tighter, my average view duration jumped. And with that, YouTube began showing my videos to audiences who had never heard of me.

Practical Editing Tips

- Trim silences and filler words.
- Add text, graphics, or cuts to re-engage attention.
- Use background music lightly to maintain energy.
- End sections with a teaser of what's next.

Action Steps

1. Analyze the retention graphs of your last three videos. Write down where drop-offs happen.
2. Script or outline your next video with a strong hook in the first 30 seconds.
3. Edit your video with pacing in mind—remove any part that doesn't serve the viewer.
4. After publishing, track retention again. Note what improved.

Closing Thoughts

Clicks may get viewers through the door, but retention keeps them inside. If your video delivers value from the start, maintains pace, and holds attention, YouTube will push it further than you expect.

6

Consistency & Upload Strategy

"*Your channel is built one brick at a time—but only if you keep laying bricks.*"

"You don't need to upload daily, but you do need to show up consistently."

My Personal Experience

When I first started, I fell into the trap of inconsistency. I'd post three videos in one week, then disappear for a month. Each time I came back, the audience had forgotten me, and YouTube stopped recommending my content.

Later, I forced myself into a rhythm: one video per week, same day, same time. Within six months, my channel gained steady traction. Why? Because consistency builds habits—not just for you, but for your viewers and for YouTube's algorithm.

I also experimented with over-uploading. For a while, I tried daily videos, thinking volume alone would guarantee growth. Instead, my quality dropped, retention fell, and burnout hit me hard. That taught me: **consistency beats frequency.**

Why Consistency Matters

- **For YouTube:** The algorithm learns your upload rhythm. It can predict when your audience expects new content and primes recommendations.
- **For Viewers:** Audiences form habits around creators they trust. If you disappear, they move on.
- **For You:** Routine eliminates procrastination and forces creative discipline.

How Often Should You Upload?

There is no one-size-fits-all answer, but here are guiding principles:

1. **Start with what you can sustain.** If one video a week is all you can manage without burning out, that's perfect.
2. **Prioritize quality over quantity.** One strong video beats five weak ones.
3. **Establish predictability.** Weekly uploads work well for most beginners. Twice a week if you have the bandwidth. Daily only if you can maintain quality.

Building an Upload Strategy

Step 1: Define Your Core Content Type

Are you making tutorials, entertainment, reviews, commentary, or vlogs? Consistency in content type helps YouTube know who to recommend you to.

Step 2: Set a Sustainable Schedule

- Beginners: 1 video per week.
- Intermediate: 2–3 per week.
- Advanced teams: daily possible, but only with support.

Step 3: Batch & Systemize

- Script or outline multiple videos at once.
- Record in batches—saves setup time.
- Edit in focused blocks.
- Schedule uploads ahead of time.

Step 4: Publish Strategically

- Post when your audience is online (check "When Your Viewers Are on YouTube" in Analytics).
- Be consistent with day and time.

The Compound Effect of Consistency

Imagine two creators:

- **Creator A:** Uploads 3 videos in a burst, then disappears for 2 months.
- **Creator B:** Uploads 1 video per week steadily for a year.

At the end of 12 months, Creator A has maybe 6–10 scattered videos. Creator B has 50. Those 50 are working 24/7, collecting clicks, building a library, and signaling to YouTube that this channel is alive and worth promoting.

Consistency compounds—like investing money. Small, steady contributions grow into something powerful over time.

Avoiding Burnout

- Don't chase daily uploads unless you have a system.
- Work in seasons—e.g., 12 weeks of steady uploads, then a 2-week break.
- Repurpose content (turn long videos into Shorts, cut highlights into clips).
- Focus on sustainable energy, not perfection.

My Turning Point

The moment I committed to one upload per week, everything changed. My audience grew slowly but surely. Comments started coming in like clockwork, because viewers trusted I would show up. Even YouTube started predicting my rhythm—recommending my videos right when new ones dropped.

It wasn't luck—it was **compounding consistency.**

Action Steps

1. Decide your realistic upload frequency (weekly, bi-weekly, or more).
2. Commit to that schedule for the next 90 days.
3. Batch 3–4 videos ahead so you never miss a week.
4. Monitor growth—not daily, but monthly.
5. Adjust only after 90 days of data.

Closing Thoughts

Consistency is not glamorous, but it's the foundation of every successful YouTube channel. A single viral hit may give you temporary growth, but consistent publishing gives you lasting momentum.

7

Audience Engagement & Community Building

"People don't subscribe to channels—they subscribe to creators they connect with."

"Views may get you discovered, but relationships keep you remembered."

My Personal Experience

When I started out, I obsessed over analytics: CTR, retention, watch time. I thought numbers alone would grow my channel. But something shifted when I began replying to comments, asking my viewers questions, and even featuring their feedback in my videos.

Suddenly, viewers weren't just watching—they were engaging. They weren't just viewers anymore; they were a **community**. They shared my content, recommended my channel to friends, and came back week after week. That's when I realized: **the algorithm may recommend your video once, but your community brings people back forever.**

Why Engagement Matters

Signal to YouTube

- Comments, likes, and shares show that viewers are emotionally invested.
- High engagement = stronger recommendation signals.

Signal to the Creator

- Engagement is feedback. It tells you what resonates and what doesn't.

Signal to the Viewer

- A channel that listens and interacts feels alive, human, and trustworthy.

Building Two-Way Conversations

- **Reply to Comments.** Even a simple "thank you" goes a long way.
- **Pin a Comment.** Use the top comment to ask a question or start a discussion.
- **Ask Questions in Videos.** Don't just present—invite feedback. Example: "Which strategy worked for you? Drop it in the comments."
- **Shoutouts.** Highlight a viewer's comment in your next video.

The Power of Names and Stories

When you remember a commenter's name and refer back in future replies, it builds loyalty. Viewers don't expect you to know them—but when you do, they feel valued.

Example:

A viewer named Raj once commented on my video about thumbnails. I mentioned his question in my next upload: "Raj asked about text size on thumbnails..." That small act made him—and dozens of others—feel this channel was a real conversation, not a one-way broadcast.

Creating a Sense of Belonging

- **Consistency + Recognition = Community.**
- Develop a signature sign-off or phrase. Viewers remember that.
- Use polls on your Community Tab to involve people in decisions.
- Run challenges (e.g., "Try this growth tip for 7 days and share your results").

Beyond the Video: Expanding Community Touchpoints

- **Community Tab.** Post updates, polls, behind-the-scenes shots.
- **Live Streams.** Interact in real time. Viewers love the raw, unedited you.
- **Shorts + Long-Form Combo.** Use Shorts to bring people in, long-form to build depth.
- **Social Media.** Instagram, Twitter, or Discord groups can extend the bond.

Engagement Without Begging

Many creators say: "Like, comment, and subscribe!" at the start of every video. But here's the truth: people act when they **feel** something, not when you beg.

Instead, trigger engagement naturally:

- Deliver value first.
- Spark curiosity.
- Leave a cliffhanger or an open-ended question.

Example: End a video with, "What's the biggest mistake you made on YouTube? I'll read your answers and maybe feature them in the next episode."

My Turning Point

The day I stopped treating YouTube like a broadcast channel and started treating it like a community hall, my growth doubled. Engagement brought momentum the algorithm alone couldn't create. My viewers became my promoters. That's the day I realized: **a loyal community is more powerful than a viral video.**

Action Steps

1. Reply to every comment on your next 5 videos.
2. Pin one engaging question as the top comment.
3. Mention at least one viewer by name in your next upload.
4. Use the Community Tab to run a poll this week.
5. Go live once a month—even if only 5 people show up.

Closing Thoughts

The algorithm may introduce you to an audience, but **engagement turns strangers into fans and fans into family.** Community is your moat—it protects your channel from being forgotten when the algorithm shifts.

8

Monetization Strategies

"*A channel without income is a hobby. A channel with income becomes a business.*"

"Your passion can stay free, but your time cannot."

My Personal Experience

When I started uploading, I only thought about views and subscribers. Money felt like a distant dream. But as I invested more time, I realized something: if YouTube was going to become a serious part of my life, it had to pay its way.

My first income wasn't from ads. It was a small brand deal—$50 to feature a product in one of my videos. It wasn't much, but it felt huge. It told me, "This is possible." Later, YouTube's AdSense kicked in, and eventually, I built multiple streams: ads, affiliate links, digital products, and services.

That journey taught me a key lesson: **don't wait for YouTube ads alone—diversify from day one.**

The 5 Core Income Streams on YouTube

1. AdSense (YouTube Partner Program)

- Requirement: 1,000 subscribers + 4,000 watch hours (or 10M Shorts views).
- Ads are the easiest entry point but usually not the biggest earner.
- RPM (Revenue per 1000 views) varies widely by niche. Finance might pay $15+, while entertainment might pay $1–2.
- Treat AdSense as **bonus money**, not your only income stream.

2. Affiliate Marketing

- Promote products you already use.
- Place affiliate links in your video descriptions.
- Example: If you teach video editing, link to your editing software, camera, or mic.
- Small channels can earn faster with affiliates than with ads.

3. Sponsorships & Brand Deals

- Brands pay you to feature their product/service.
- Even with 5,000–10,000 subscribers, you can get deals if your niche is specific.
- Charge based on audience quality, not just size.
- Build a media kit (channel stats, audience demographics, past examples).

4. Digital Products

- Ebooks, online courses, templates, presets, or coaching.
- These scale better than physical products and require no inventory.
- Example: "YouTube Thumbnail Pack," "Beginner's Video Editing Course," "30-Day YouTube Growth Plan."

5. Community Support

- Channel memberships, Patreon, or paid live streams.
- Works best when you already have a loyal, engaged audience.
- Offer perks like behind-the-scenes content, Q&A sessions, or exclusive templates.

The Monetization Pyramid

Think of income like a pyramid:

- **Base Layer:** Ads and affiliates (easy to start, low control).
- **Middle Layer:** Sponsorships (medium effort, bigger payouts).
- **Top Layer:** Your own products/services (high effort, maximum control).

Long-term success comes from building **all three layers**.

Pricing Yourself for Sponsorships

A common mistake: undervaluing.

- Rough guide: $15–$30 per 1,000 views (depending on niche).
- Example: If your video averages 10,000 views, a fair deal might be $200–$300.
- If your niche is high-value (finance, tech, marketing), you can charge more.
- Don't just sell "views"—sell **access to a specific audience**.

My Turning Point

When I sold my first digital product—a simple ebook on content strategy—I realized I didn't need millions of views to earn real income. Just 50 buyers at $10 each gave me $500 in a week. That was more than months of AdSense at the time.

That moment taught me: **your biggest opportunity is not views—it's trust.** When viewers trust you, they'll invest in what you create.

Action Steps

1. Join the YouTube Partner Program once you qualify—but don't wait for it.
2. Add one affiliate link today for a product you already use.
3. Start a simple media kit (audience stats + what value you offer brands).
4. Brainstorm one digital product your audience would pay for.
5. Build one "community support" option (Patreon, memberships, or live sessions).

Closing Thoughts

Monetization is not a single switch; it's a system. AdSense is just the beginning, but the real power lies in diversifying your income. When you combine ads, affiliates, sponsors, and your own offers, YouTube shifts from being just a platform into a **sustainable business.**

9

Analytics & Data-Driven Growth

"What gets measured, gets improved."

"Data is not the enemy of creativity—it's the map that guides it."

My Personal Experience

When I first opened YouTube Analytics, I was overwhelmed. Graphs, numbers, acronyms everywhere—CTR, AVD, RPM. I felt like I needed a degree in statistics to understand any of it. So, like many creators, I ignored it and just kept posting blindly.

But here's what happened: some videos grew, others died, and I had no idea why. Only when I started studying analytics did I realize that YouTube was handing me the answers the whole time. The numbers weren't there to confuse me—they were showing me **what my audience liked, what they skipped, and what they wanted more of.**

The day I understood my retention graph, I stopped guessing. That's when my channel shifted from "random uploads" to "intentional growth."

Why Analytics Matter

- **For You:** Analytics show you what's working and what's wasting your time.
- **For YouTube:** Data tells the platform your audience's behavior, which shapes recommendations.
- **For Growth:** Small insights—like when viewers drop off—can transform your next video.

The 5 Metrics That Actually Matter

Forget drowning in numbers. Focus on these five pillars:

CTR (Click-Through Rate)

- Measures: How many impressions turned into clicks.
- Why it matters: Weak CTR = your video never gets a chance.
- Fix: Better titles and thumbnails (see Chapter 4).

Average View Duration (AVD)

- Measures: How long the average viewer watches.
- Why it matters: Shows how engaging your content is.
- Fix: Stronger hooks, faster pacing, tighter editing.

Audience Retention Graph

- Measures: Where viewers stay, rewatch, or drop off.
- Why it matters: Pinpoints exactly where you're losing attention.
- Fix: Re-edit intros, add open loops, cut filler.

Traffic Sources

- Measures: Where viewers find your video (Search, Browse, Suggested, Shorts feed).
- Why it matters: Reveals if your content is optimized for discovery or recommendation.
- Fix: Adjust titles, thumbnails, and topics to align with desired traffic.

Subscribers Gained vs Lost

- Measures: Net growth from each video.
- Why it matters: Tells you which videos are turning viewers into loyal fans.
- Fix: Double down on content types that drive subs.

Secondary Metrics (Useful, but Don't Obsess)

- **RPM/CPM:** Helpful for monetization, but doesn't drive growth.
- **Shares:** Nice indicator, but not the primary growth driver.
- **Likes:** Positive feedback, but weaker than watch time/retention.

My Turning Point

One of my videos had 100,000 impressions but only 2,000 views. That's when I realized the CTR was killing me. I redesigned the thumbnail and rewrote the title. Within 72 hours, views tripled.

Another time, I noticed a massive drop at 45 seconds in one video. Why? I had inserted a 20-second irrelevant story. Next upload, I cut filler. Retention jumped.

Analytics aren't cold numbers—they're feedback straight from your viewers.

Building a Data-Driven Workflow

After Upload (First 24–72 hours):

- Check CTR and retention. Is the video getting clicks? Are people staying?

After 1–2 Weeks:

- Study traffic sources. Did the video rank in Search, or get recommended?

Monthly Review:

- Identify top 3 performers. Ask: What do they have in common?
- Identify bottom 3. Ask: What do they lack?

Quarterly Strategy Reset:

- Double down on formats/topics that drive growth.
- Drop experiments that repeatedly underperform.

How to Read Retention Like a Pro

- **Sharp drop at 0–30 seconds:** Weak hook. Redesign your intros.
- **Gradual decline:** Natural, but tighten pacing to slow the fall.
- **Rewatch spikes:** Something valuable or entertaining happened. Use it again.
- **Flat retention near the end:** Perfect! You're holding attention. Consider adding a call-to-action (like watching another video).

Tools & Tricks

- **YouTube Studio Mobile App:** Quick daily checks.
- **Advanced Mode (Desktop):** Deep dive into traffic, geography, and playback device.
- **Compare Feature:** Overlay two videos' graphs to see why one outper-

formed the other.

Action Steps

1. Open your last 5 videos. Write down CTR, AVD, and retention drop-off points.
2. For the worst-performing one, redesign title/thumbnail and re-upload as a test.
3. For the best-performing one, study traffic sources and replicate the winning formula.
4. Set a weekly "analytics check-in" for 30 minutes—no more, no less.
5. Track progress in a simple spreadsheet to see patterns over time.

Closing Thoughts

Analytics are not about perfection. They're about progress. Each number tells a story about what your audience loves and what they ignore. When you respect the data and act on it, your channel evolves from guesswork into a growth machine.

10

Collaboration & Networking

"*If you want to go fast, go alone. If you want to go far, go together.*"

"Collaboration is the shortcut to audiences you could never reach alone."

My Personal Experience

For a long time, I tried to do everything solo—record, edit, upload, promote. I thought success on YouTube was a one-man show. But then I collaborated with another creator in my niche. He had an audience that didn't know me, and I had insights his viewers wanted.

That single collaboration exposed me to thousands of new people overnight. Many subscribed, not because of algorithms, but because of trust. His audience trusted him, so when he introduced me, I inherited that trust. That was the day I learned: **networking grows not just your reach, but your reputation.**

Why Collaboration Works

Shared Trust

- Audiences trust creators they already follow. A collaboration is a recommendation by default.

Cross-Pollination

- You borrow each other's audiences. One plus one becomes more than two.

Content Energy

- Collaboration videos often feel fresh and engaging—two personalities create better dynamics.

Relationship Building

- Opportunities multiply when you have peers, not just competitors.

Types of Collaborations

Guest Appearances

- Appear on another creator's video for a segment.
- Example: A guest Q&A, debate, or expert tip.

Co-Creation

- Film a full video together.
- Example: Two creators tackling the same challenge or sharing different strategies.

Shoutouts & Mentions

- A simple endorsement in your video or theirs.
- Example: "Check out [channel]—they did a brilliant breakdown of this same topic."

Playlist & Series

- Build a mini-series across both channels.
- Example: Part 1 on your channel, Part 2 on theirs.

Live Streams

- Go live together and share audiences in real time.

Finding the Right Partners

- Look for **aligned niches, not identical ones.**
- Example: A video editor can collaborate with a filmmaker or a productivity coach.
- Aim for **similar audience size.** Big creators rarely collab with tiny ones unless there's unique value.
- Focus on **audience overlap.** If their viewers could benefit from your content, it's a good fit.

How to Approach Collaborations

Do Your Homework

- Watch their content. Know their style and audience.

Offer Value First

- Don't just say, "Collab with me." Suggest how the collaboration benefits *their* viewers.

Keep it Simple

- Start with small gestures: mention them, comment on their videos, share their work.

Build Relationships, Not Transactions

- Networking is long-term. Some of my best collabs happened months after the first connection.

Beyond YouTube: Networking Channels

- **Social Media (Twitter, LinkedIn, Instagram):** Engage with creators outside the platform.
- **Communities & Forums:** Discord groups, Facebook groups, Reddit subs.
- **Events & Conferences:** Meeting in person accelerates trust.

My Turning Point

After my first successful collaboration, I stopped seeing other creators as competition. I began reaching out, joining online groups, and even offering free help. The more I gave, the more came back. Opportunities snowballed.

11

The Future of YouTube & Adapting to Change

"The only constant in life is change." – Heraclitus

"On YouTube, survival doesn't go to the biggest creator—it goes to the one who adapts fastest."

My Personal Experience

When I first started on YouTube, things were simple: you made videos, added a few tags, and if people liked them, they spread. Then came algorithm changes, Shorts, stricter policies, monetization requirements, new features like Community posts. Every time YouTube introduced something new, I felt like I was starting over.

At first, I resisted. I told myself, "I'll just keep doing what I've always done." But soon, I noticed my views dropping while others who embraced new features surged ahead. That's when I learned the golden rule: **YouTube rewards adaptability.**

The creators who experiment with new tools, formats, and trends early are the ones who stay ahead.

The Nature of Change on YouTube

- **Algorithm Updates:** Priorities shift (e.g., watch time → session time → Shorts engagement).
- **Feature Rollouts:** Shorts, Stories, Community tab, Shopping integration, AI tools.
- **Audience Behavior:** Viewer habits change—attention spans shorten, devices evolve.
- **Monetization Shifts:** From ads to memberships, Super Thanks, affiliate links, brand deals.

What Change Really Means

Change is not a threat. Change is YouTube's way of rewarding creators who evolve. Each new update opens opportunities:

- When Shorts launched, small creators exploded overnight.
- When live streaming became popular, creators built stronger communities.
- When Community posts rolled out, channels engaged viewers even without uploads.

Those who embraced change grew. Those who resisted stayed stuck.

The Mindset of Adaptability

Curiosity over Fear

- Instead of "What if this hurts my channel?", ask, "How can I use this to my advantage?"

Experimentation over Perfection

- Test new formats, even if they're not polished. The winners are discovered through trying.

Flexibility over Stubbornness

- Don't get emotionally attached to one format. Viewers change; you should too.

Current & Emerging Trends to Watch

Short-Form Content

- Shorts are no longer optional—they're a growth rocket. Expect more monetization and tools around them.

AI & Automation

- From auto-subtitles to AI-generated music, creators who learn to use these tools will save time and create more.

Creator Economy Expansion

- Memberships, Super Thanks, and brand deals are becoming as important as ad revenue.

Interactive Content

- Polls, quizzes, clickable CTAs inside videos—expect more ways to engage audiences directly.

Shopping & E-commerce

- YouTube is testing in-video product tagging. The line between content and commerce will blur.

My Turning Point

I remember resisting Shorts at first. "They're just TikTok copies," I told myself. But once I tried them, I saw my subscriber growth triple in weeks. Many of those new viewers later became long-form video watchers.

That was my lesson: the future doesn't ask for your permission—it rewards your participation.

How to Future-Proof Your Channel

Stay Educated

- Follow YouTube's official Creator Insider channel and blog for updates.

Diversify Formats

- Don't rely on just one type of content. Mix long-form, Shorts, live streams, and community posts.

Build a Brand, Not Just Videos

- Strong personal branding ensures you survive algorithm shifts. People follow *you*, not just the content.

Own Your Audience

- Collect emails or build a presence outside YouTube (Instagram, website, Discord). That way, you're not 100% at the mercy of algorithm changes.

Adapt Quickly

- When YouTube launches something new, don't wait—experiment immediately. Early adopters often get the biggest rewards.

Action Steps

1. Identify one new YouTube feature (Shorts, Community tab, live, Shopping) and start experimenting this month.
2. Watch analytics closely—see how audiences respond to new formats.
3. Follow at least 2–3 industry experts or channels that discuss YouTube updates.
4. Begin building an email list or Discord group to secure your audience outside YouTube.
5. Every quarter, review your channel strategy and ask: "Am I adapting or resisting?"

Closing Thoughts

YouTube will never stop evolving. Neither should you. The creators who last for years are not always the most talented or the luckiest—they are the most adaptable.

The future belongs to those who learn, adjust, and act quickly. If you embrace this mindset, no update will ever scare you again.

12

Bringing It All Together (Your Roadmap to YouTube Success)

"Success is the sum of small efforts, repeated day in and day out." – Robert Collier

"YouTube success is not luck, it's a system—and now you have the roadmap."

My Personal Experience

When I look back at my own YouTube journey, I see years of trial, error, frustration, and small wins that eventually turned into big breakthroughs. There were nights when I questioned if it was worth it. Days when I uploaded videos that got less than 50 views and felt invisible.

But what kept me going was one belief: **consistency and learning always pay off.** I didn't need one viral video to change everything—I needed steady growth, smart strategy, and resilience. And over time, that's exactly what happened.

This book is not just about algorithms, titles, or monetization. It's about giving you a system—a way to approach YouTube with clarity and confidence, instead of guessing and hoping.

Your Roadmap to YouTube Success

Let's tie all the chapters together into a step-by-step framework:
Step 1: Master the Foundation

- Know why you're creating content (Chapter 1: The Creator's Mindset).
- Understand how the YouTube algorithm works (Chapter 2).

Step 2: Build Discoverable Content

- Research and create content around demand (Chapter 3: Content Creation).
- Design irresistible titles and thumbnails (Chapter 4: CTR).

Step 3: Keep Viewers Watching

- Focus on watch time and retention strategies (Chapter 5).
- Stick to a consistent upload schedule (Chapter 6).

Step 4: Build Relationships, Not Just Views

- Engage deeply with your audience (Chapter 7).
- Turn viewers into a loyal community.

Step 5: Monetize Smartly

- Diversify income: ads, brand deals, memberships, and more (Chapter 8).

Step 6: Let Data Guide You

- Use analytics to measure, adapt, and grow (Chapter 9).

Step 7: Expand Through People

- Collaborate and network to multiply your reach (Chapter 10).

Step 8: Stay Ahead of the Curve

- Adapt to trends and future-proof your channel (Chapter 11).

The Big Picture

When you put all of this together, you'll realize YouTube isn't about luck. It's about:

- **Clarity** (knowing your niche, your audience, your goals).
- **Consistency** (showing up even when it feels slow).
- **Adaptability** (embracing change instead of fearing it).
- **Community** (treating viewers as people, not numbers).
- **Persistence** (because growth takes time, but the rewards compound).

My Final Advice

Play the Long Game

- Don't chase shortcuts. Focus on building a channel that lasts years, not weeks.

Balance Creativity with Strategy

- Passion fuels your content, but data directs your growth. Use both.

Measure Progress, Not Perfection

- Every subscriber, every comment, every improved retention graph is a victory.

Never Stop Learning

- YouTube will keep evolving. Stay curious, stay humble, stay hungry.

Remember Why You Started

- At the end of the day, YouTube is about sharing something you care about with the world. Never lose that spark.

Action Steps: Your First 90 Days

- **Week 1–2:** Define your niche, set up your channel, plan 10 video ideas.
- **Week 3–4:** Create and upload your first 2–3 videos. Don't aim for perfect—just publish.
- **Month 2:** Focus on improving titles, thumbnails, and retention. Start studying analytics.
- **Month 3:** Engage with your audience, experiment with Shorts, and plan your first collaboration.
- By Day 90, you'll already see patterns—what works, what doesn't, and how to grow smarter.

Closing Thoughts

YouTube is not just a platform—it's a journey of self-discovery, discipline, and impact. Every creator you admire once stood where you are now: small, uncertain, but full of potential.

The difference between those who quit and those who succeed is not talent—

it's persistence, learning, and adaptability.

So my final message to you is this: **your voice matters. Your story matters. The world is waiting. Start creating, keep learning, and never stop.**

Because one day, someone will look at your channel and say, "This creator changed my life."

And that will make every struggle worth it.

13

Decoding the Hidden Signals of the YouTube Algorithm

"Don't chase views. Chase satisfaction—and the algorithm will chase you."

"The secret is not to beat the algorithm—it's to align with it."

My Personal Experience

When I first started, I thought the algorithm was my enemy. Every time my video flopped, I'd complain: "The algorithm hates me!" But over time, I realized something powerful: **the algorithm doesn't hate or love anyone—it simply reflects how viewers respond.**

The day I understood that was a turning point. I stopped blaming YouTube and started studying what made viewers click, watch, and feel satisfied. That's when my channel shifted from frustration to steady growth.

The Truth About the Algorithm

YouTube's algorithm is not a mystery—it's a **system built to maximize viewer satisfaction.** Its ultimate goal is simple:

- Keep people watching.
- Keep them coming back.
- Keep them happy with what they watch.

If your videos help YouTube achieve those goals, the algorithm will promote you.

The Hidden Signals YouTube Tracks

Click-Through Rate (CTR)

- Are people choosing your video when shown?
- High CTR tells YouTube: *"This video looks interesting."*

Watch Time & Retention

- Do viewers stay, or drop off quickly?
- Strong retention says: *"This video delivers on its promise."*

Session Time

- Do viewers keep watching YouTube after your video?
- If yes, YouTube rewards you for keeping users on the platform.

Engagement (Likes, Comments, Shares, Saves)

- Engagement = investment. It signals deeper satisfaction.

Satisfaction Surveys (Yes, YouTube actually asks viewers)

- "Were you satisfied with this recommendation?"
- YouTube quietly uses this data to improve personalization.

Consistency of Uploads

- Regular uploads teach YouTube: *"This channel is reliable."*

The Personalization Factor

Here's something many creators forget: **the algorithm doesn't treat all viewers equally.**

- Your video may explode in one region but flop in another.
- One viewer may see your video on their home feed, another may never see it.
- Why? Because YouTube tailors recommendations to *individual behavior.*

That means your job is not to please everyone—it's to please your *target audience* so well that YouTube knows exactly who to recommend you to.

My Turning Point

I had one video that performed horribly at first. CTR was low, watch time was decent, but it wasn't spreading. I almost gave up.

Then, weeks later, I noticed traffic picking up. Why? YouTube finally figured out *who the video was for.* Once it started showing it to the right audience, views skyrocketed.

Lesson learned: **sometimes it's not your content that's wrong—it's about giving the algorithm enough signals to match your video with the right viewers.**

How to Align With the Algorithm

Hook Viewers Quickly

- Your first 15 seconds decide if people stay.

Deliver What You Promise

- Don't mislead with clickbait—YouTube punishes high drop-offs.

Encourage Deeper Engagement

- Ask questions in your video so viewers comment.
- Suggest playlists so they keep watching.

Experiment & Track

- Use analytics (Chapter 9) to see where retention drops.
- Test different thumbnails and titles for CTR.

Think "Viewer Journey," Not Just One Video

- Your video should lead to another video of yours, creating a viewing loop.

Action Steps

1. Open YouTube Studio → Analytics → Reach tab. Study your CTR vs average.
2. Open the Engagement tab → Check where viewers drop off in retention.
3. Create one playlist this week that groups related videos together.
4. Add a question or poll in your next video to boost engagement.
5. Track results for 30 days—see how hidden signals change over time.

Closing Thoughts

The algorithm isn't a monster in the shadows—it's a mirror reflecting your audience's behavior. When viewers are satisfied, YouTube rewards you automatically.

So stop asking, "How do I beat the algorithm?" and start asking, **"How do I delight my audience?"**

Because when your audience wins, YouTube wins—and then you win too.

14

Case Studies of the World's Top Creators

"Success leaves clues—study the greats, and you'll find your path."

"The world's biggest creators weren't born famous—they built systems, brick by brick, just like you can."

Why Study Case Studies?

When we see a creator with 50 million subscribers, it feels impossible—like they live in another world. But the truth is, every successful YouTuber started with zero. By studying their strategies, habits, and mistakes, we can find **patterns of success** that apply even if we're just beginning.

I've personally spent hours breaking down the journeys of some of the most influential YouTubers in the world. Here's what I discovered.

Case Study 1: MrBeast (Jimmy Donaldson) – Retention is Everything

- **Background:** Started posting at age 13. Early content? Random gameplay and skits—nothing viral.
- **Breakthrough:** Obsession with data. He and his friends studied thousands of videos, retention graphs, and titles.
- **Core Strategy:** Extreme storytelling + massive reinvestment into production.
- **Key Lessons for You:**

Retention is king—he hooks you in the first 5 seconds.

Always reinvest—he put every dollar back into making bigger, better videos.

Think bigger—his ideas scale far beyond ordinary content.

Takeaway: You don't need millions to start, but you do need to focus on **retention** and **value reinvestment** (time, money, or creativity).

Case Study 2: PewDiePie (Felix Kjellberg) – Authenticity Wins

- **Background:** Started with gaming commentary in his bedroom. Grew into the most-subscribed creator at his peak.
- **Breakthrough:** Staying relatable, authentic, and evolving his content style.
- **Core Strategy:** Personality-first content—his fans followed *him*, not just the games.
- **Key Lessons for You:**

Be yourself—authenticity builds loyalty.

1. Don't be afraid to pivot—he moved from gaming → memes → commentary → lifestyle.
2. Your community matters—his fans became his biggest promoters.

Takeaway: You don't need to "act big"—you just need to be real and build trust.

Case Study 3: Marques Brownlee (MKBHD) – Quality Over Quantity

- **Background:** Started as a teenager, filming gadget reviews on a webcam.
- **Breakthrough:** Commitment to high production value and deep knowledge.
- **Core Strategy:** Polished videos + consistency + credibility in tech.
- **Key Lessons for You:**

Focus on quality—viewers trust creators who respect their time.

Become an expert—authority builds influence.

Don't rush—slow, steady growth beats viral spikes.

Takeaway: Even in crowded niches, professionalism and passion stand out.

Case Study 4: Emma Chamberlain – Connection Over Perfection

- **Background:** Teenager who posted quirky, unpolished lifestyle videos.
- **Breakthrough:** Authentic editing style (jump cuts, randomness, imperfections) that made her feel relatable.
- **Core Strategy:** Relatable personality, not polished production.
- **Key Lessons for You:**

Imperfections are human—don't wait until you have the best gear.

Build emotional connection, not cinematic beauty.

Being different is often better than being perfect.

Takeaway: You don't need perfect videos—you need *personal connection.*

Case Study 5: CarryMinati (Ajey Nagar) - Cultural Relevance

- **Background:** Indian creator who began with gaming and later shifted to roast/commentary.
- **Breakthrough:** Blended humor, relatability, and timing with trending topics.
- **Core Strategy:** Speak the language of his audience—literally and culturally.
- **Key Lessons for You:**

Know your audience deeply—inside jokes, local culture, and trends.

Jump on trends quickly—speed matters.

Stay original within your niche—his style is hard to replicate.

Takeaway: Global rules apply, but *local connection wins hearts.*

My Reflections

When I studied these creators, I realized they all had different approaches—big budgets, small budgets, polished or raw—but one common thread united them:

- **They knew their audience.**

- **They committed long-term.**
- **They adapted constantly.**

That's the real formula, and it's something every creator—including you—can apply today.

Action Steps

1. Pick 3 creators in your niche and study their top 10 videos.
2. Note their title styles, hooks, retention strategies, and how they engage with their audience.
3. Ask: *"How can I apply this in my way, with my resources?"*
4. Create one video this month inspired by your research, but with your personal twist.

Closing Thoughts

Big creators may feel out of reach, but they started exactly where you are now. Their journeys prove that **strategy + persistence + adaptability = success.**

If they could do it, so can you. The only difference is—will you stay consistent long enough to see it through?

15

Overcoming Burnout & Staying Creative Long-Term

"Success is not about never getting tired—it's about learning how to keep going when you are."

"Even the biggest YouTubers hit walls—what matters is how you climb over them."

My Personal Experience

I remember the first time I felt true burnout. I had been uploading consistently, chasing growth, pouring my heart into editing, but the numbers didn't match my effort. Views were stuck. Income was small. I felt like shouting: *"Why am I doing all this?"*

For a while, I lost my spark. I uploaded out of duty, not joy. And it showed—my energy dipped, my creativity dried up, and my audience felt it too.

But then I realized something powerful: **burnout isn't a sign you're weak—it's a signal that you need to adjust.**

Why Burnout Happens

Burnout is common in creators, and it usually comes from:

1. **Unrealistic expectations** – expecting viral growth too fast.
2. **Overwork without balance** – editing at 3 AM, skipping rest.
3. **Chasing metrics, not meaning** – living and dying by view counts.
4. **Comparison trap** – measuring yourself against bigger creators.

The truth? Burnout doesn't mean you should quit—it means you need to redesign your process.

Lessons From Top Creators

- **MrBeast:** Took multiple breaks when his health and mind needed rest, but came back stronger.
- **Emma Chamberlain:** Stepped away from YouTube for months, focused on herself, then returned with even more impact.
- **Ali Abdaal:** Talks openly about balancing content creation with a sustainable lifestyle.

Even the giants step back sometimes. That doesn't make them less successful—it makes them *human.*

How I Bounced Back

What saved me wasn't pushing harder—it was slowing down. I set new rules for myself:

- I batched content so I wasn't always editing last-minute.
- I created an "idea bank" so I never stared at a blank screen.
- I set a schedule I could actually sustain.
- Most importantly, I reconnected with *why* I started creating—to share, to help, to express—not just to chase numbers.

Slowly, my energy returned. My creativity came back. And ironically, my channel started growing faster.

Practical Ways to Avoid Burnout

Batch Your Content

- Film 2–3 videos in one sitting. Edit over time.
- This reduces constant pressure.

Create an Idea Bank

- Keep a running list (Google Docs, Notion, or even a notebook).
- Anytime you feel low-energy, pull from the list.

Set a Realistic Schedule

- Don't promise "daily videos" if you can't sustain it.
- Consistency matters more than frequency.

Take Creative Breaks

- Watch movies, read, travel—refuel your brain.
- Inspiration often comes when you step away.

Celebrate Small Wins

- Don't just celebrate 1M views—celebrate your first 100 subscribers, your first comment that says "You helped me."

Focus on Your 'Why'

- Write down why you started.
- Revisit that note when numbers feel discouraging.

Action Steps

1. This week, create an "Idea Bank" with at least 20 video ideas.
2. Set a realistic upload schedule (e.g., 1 video per week). Stick to it for 90 days.
3. Block out one day per month as a "creative rest day"—no content, just inspiration.
4. Write your personal "why" on a sticky note and keep it near your desk.

Closing Thoughts

Burnout is not the end—it's a checkpoint. Every creator faces it. The difference between those who quit and those who succeed is simple: **resilience.**

If you learn how to rest, refocus, and reconnect with your purpose, you'll not only outlast burnout—you'll become stronger because of it.

Remember: this is not a sprint. YouTube is a marathon. If you pace yourself right, your creativity will last for years—and so will your success.

16

Final Words: Your Journey Begins Now

If you've made it this far, let me pause and say—thank you. Thank you for investing your time, your focus, and your heart into reading this book. Out of billions of people in the world, you chose to be a creator. That decision alone makes you rare.

Here's the truth: YouTube success isn't about algorithms, titles, thumbnails, or even equipment. Those are tools. The real engine of your growth will always be **you**—your voice, your consistency, your resilience.

I want you to remember this: every creator you admire once stood exactly where you are today. Zero subscribers. Zero views. Zero revenue. The only difference between them and those who quit is that they *kept going.*

The road ahead won't always be easy. You'll face days of doubt, videos that flop, maybe even months that feel stuck. But if you apply what you've learned here—step by step, with patience and purpose—you will grow. Maybe not overnight, but over time, in ways bigger than you can imagine.

And when you finally upload that video that changes everything—the one that reaches thousands, maybe millions—I hope you'll smile and think back to this moment. The moment you decided not just to dream, but to act.

So go create. Be consistent. Be brave. Be yourself. And remember: you're not just building a channel—you're building a legacy.

Your journey starts now. I'll see you on the other side of success.
Tarun Takshay

17

The 90-Day YouTube Growth Blueprint

Core secrets and growth codes to go from 0 to 1 Million fast

Phase 1: Days 1–30 (Laying the Foundation)

- **Set up your channel the right way**
- Clear name, professional logo/banner, about page optimized.
- Niche selection: pick ONE problem, passion, or audience type.
- **Research before you record**
- Study top 10 channels in your niche.
- Collect 50+ content ideas by spying on what's already working.
- **Upload your first 4–6 videos**
- Focus on clarity, not perfection.
- Use proven title structures (How to..., Top 10..., Vs..., Secret of...).

Code Thought #1: *Don't reinvent the wheel—model what works, then add your unique twist.*

Phase 2: Days 31–60 (Building Momentum)

- **Consistency lock-in**
- Minimum 2 videos per week, same day/time.

- Create a content calendar.
- **Thumbnail + Title mastery**
- Test 2–3 designs per video; watch CTR analytics.
- **Engagement hacks**
- End every video with 1 specific call to comment.
- Use pinned comments to spark discussion.
- **Cross-promotion**
- Share in relevant Facebook groups, Instagram, or collaborations with micro-creators.

Code Thought #2: *Engagement fuels growth—comments and likes are free "ads" to the algorithm.*

Phase 3: Days 61–90 (Explosion Phase)

- **Double down on winners**
- Check analytics: which 20% of your videos are driving 80% of growth?
- Make follow-ups, sequels, spin-offs of those topics.
- **Playlists & Binge Factor**
- Arrange videos into playlists with compelling titles ("Watch this first," "Step-by-step guide").
- Link one video to the next to trap viewers in your ecosystem.
- **Collaboration & Networking**
- Appear on other channels—even small ones.
- Leverage shorts to push discoverability.
- **Monetization prep**
- Enable ads once eligible.
- Add affiliate links or product mentions.

Code Thought #3: *The fastest growth comes from doubling down on what already works—not chasing random ideas.*

Core Secrets Revealed

Hook + Retention > Everything

- Viral growth depends on people *staying*.

Your First 1000 True Fans Matter More Than 1M Views

- Focus on depth, not vanity metrics.

Consistency Creates Compounding Growth

- Every video is a soldier working for you 24/7.

Speed Beats Perfection

- Upload fast, learn fast, adjust fast.

Money Follows Value

- Serve your audience → the algorithm serves you → revenue follows.

The Million-Subscriber Mindset

Hitting a million isn't just strategy—it's identity. Act like a million-subscriber creator from day one:

- Show up professionally.
- Treat your viewers like a community.
- Invest time and energy as if success is guaranteed.

Because once you think, plan, and act like a million-subscriber creator, the numbers eventually catch up.

18

From 0 to 1 Million Subscribers Blueprints

F*rom 0 to 1 Million Subscribers—Core Secrets & Action Codes*

"You don't need a thousand strategies—just ninety days of relentless focus."

"This is the playbook I wish I had when I started from zero."

Phase 1: Days 1–30 – Laying the Foundation

Week 1: Setting Up Like a Pro

- Create/optimize your channel: name, logo, banner, About section.
- Write a mission statement: *"This channel helps [audience] achieve [result]."*
- Research your niche: list 10 successful channels + their top 5 videos.

Week 2: Content Bank Creation

- Brainstorm 50+ video ideas.
- Organize into 3 categories: evergreen, trending, personal story.
- Choose your first 6 video topics.

Week 3: First Uploads

- Film and upload 2–3 simple but clear videos.
- Don't obsess over quality—focus on clarity and completion.
- Use proven title formats:
- "How to [achieve result] in [time]"
- "Top 5 Mistakes in [niche]"
- "[Secret/Truth] Nobody Tells You About [topic]"

Week 4: Analytics Kickoff

- Open YouTube Studio daily: track CTR, watch time, and comments.
- Take notes: what thumbnails/titles perform best?
- Upload 2 more videos.

Code Thought #1: *Imperfect action beats perfect hesitation. Just upload.*

Phase 2: Days 31–60 – Building Momentum

Week 5: Consistency Lock-In

- Commit to 2 videos per week, same day/time.
- Build a content calendar (Google Sheets or Notion).

Week 6: Engagement Mastery

- End each video with 1 specific call-to-action:
- "Comment your biggest struggle..."
- "Which of these tips helped you most?"
- Pin your own comment and reply to every viewer.

Week 7: Thumbnail + Title Testing

- Create 2 versions of a thumbnail → run A/B test.
- Study analytics: which version gets higher CTR?
- Keep iterating until CTR is above niche average.

Week 8: Cross-Promotion Hacks

- Share videos in niche Facebook groups, Reddit, and Instagram Stories.
- Network with 2–3 micro-creators and exchange shoutouts.
- Upload your first **Shorts** for discovery.

Code Thought #2: *Engagement is the free fuel of the algorithm—spark it daily.*

Phase 3: Days 61-90 - The Explosion Phase

Week 9: Doubling Down on Winners

- Check analytics: identify top 3 videos.
- Make sequels, deeper dives, or follow-up videos on those topics.
- Repurpose those videos into Shorts.

Week 10: Playlists & Binge Factor

- Organize videos into playlists with enticing names:
- "Start Here"
- "Secrets of [Niche]"
- "Step-by-Step Growth"
- Add playlist links in end screens and descriptions.

Week 11: Collaboration Power

- Reach out to 5 creators in your niche (small or big).
- Do a collab video, guest interview, or reaction video.
- Appear on podcasts or Instagram Lives to expand reach.

Week 12: Monetization Prep

- If eligible, enable AdSense.
- Add affiliate links or digital product mentions.
- Create a free lead magnet (guide, checklist) to start email list.

Code Thought #3: *The fastest growth comes from doubling down on what already works, not chasing random ideas.*

Core Secrets to Growth

1. **Hook + Retention = Viral Growth**

- CTR gets you clicks, retention keeps you in recommendations.

1. **Focus on First 1,000 Fans**

- Loyal viewers → bigger than 1M random views.

1. **Consistency Compounds**

- Every video is a soldier—upload often, and your army grows.

1. **Speed Over Perfection**

- Done is better than perfect. Adjust after publishing.

1. **Serve Before You Sell**

- Give value → audience grows → money flows.

Mindset for 1 Million Subscribers

- **Act like you already have 1M subs.**
- Professional branding, clear messaging, high energy.
- **Be obsessed with your audience, not the algorithm.**
- The algorithm follows the audience anyway.
- **Stay patient and persistent.**
- 90 days can skyrocket growth, but the real game is lifelong.

Final Action Plan Checklist (Print This Out)

✅ Channel set up professionally
✅ 50+ content ideas ready
✅ 12+ videos uploaded in 90 days
✅ CTR tested and optimized
✅ Playlists created and optimized
✅ Collab with at least 1 creator
✅ Monetization system started
✅ "Why" statement visible at desk

Closing Note

If you follow this 90-day blueprint with relentless consistency, you won't just grow a YouTube channel—you'll transform into a creator with unstoppable momentum. Whether you hit 1 million in 90 days or 100K in a year, the habits you build here are the real treasure.

Remember: numbers are just milestones. The real victory is becoming the kind of person who doesn't give up, no matter what.

19

90-Day YouTube Growth Calendar (Week-by-Week Action Plan)

Phase 1: Days 1–30 – Laying the Foundation

Week 1: Channel Setup & Research

- Create/optimize channel (logo, banner, About section).
- Write mission statement ("This channel helps [audience] achieve [result]").
- Research 10 successful channels in your niche.
- Study their top 5 videos for patterns (titles, thumbnails, retention).

Week 2: Content Bank Creation

- Brainstorm 50+ video ideas.
- Divide into Evergreen, Trending, and Personal Story categories.
- Pick your first 6 ideas.

Week 3: First Uploads

- Film and upload 2–3 videos (clarity > perfection).

- Use proven title formats ("How to...", "Top 5...", "Secrets of...").
- Start building your description template (with keywords + CTAs).

Week 4: Analytics Kickoff

- Upload 2 more videos.
- Check analytics daily: CTR, watch time, comments.
- Take notes: what worked? what didn't?

Phase 2: Days 31–60 – Building Momentum

Week 5: Consistency Lock-In

- Commit to 2 videos/week (set upload days/times).
- Build content calendar for next 30 days.

Week 6: Engagement Mastery

- Add a clear call-to-action in every video.
- Pin your own comment.
- Reply to every viewer comment.

Week 7: Thumbnail + Title Testing

- Create at least 2 thumbnail variations.
- Use A/B testing or swap after 48 hours.
- Aim for CTR above niche average.

Week 8: Cross-Promotion Hacks

- Share videos in 3–5 niche communities (FB, Reddit, Instagram).
- Collaborate with at least 1 micro-creator.
- Upload your first Shorts for discoverability.

Phase 3: Days 61–90 – Explosion Phase
Week 9: Double Down on Winners

- Identify top 3 videos by views/retention.
- Make sequels, spin-offs, or updates.
- Repurpose content into Shorts.

Week 10: Playlists & Binge Factor

- Create 3+ playlists with compelling names.
- Add end screens linking to next video.
- Organize descriptions with playlist links.

Week 11: Collaboration Power

- Reach out to 5 creators in your niche.
- Record 1 collaboration or guest feature.
- Appear on 1 podcast/IG Live for exposure.

Week 12: Monetization Prep

- Enable AdSense (if eligible).
- Add affiliate links or test digital product mentions.
- Create a free resource (PDF, guide) to start email list.

Quick Recap Checklist

✅ Channel optimized professionally
✅ 50+ content ideas ready
✅ 12–15 videos uploaded in 90 days
✅ CTR tested and improved
✅ Playlists created and optimized
✅ At least 1 collaboration completed

✅ Monetization system prepared
✅ "Why" statement written & visible

20

YouTube Growth in 90 Days – Cheat Sheet

Your fast-track roadmap from 0 to 1 Million

Phase 1: Days 1–30 – Foundation

- ✅ Optimize channel (logo, banner, About section, mission statement).
- ✅ Research top 10 channels in your niche + note winning patterns.
- ✅ Create 50+ video ideas (Evergreen, Trending, Personal).
- ✅ Upload first 4–6 videos (clarity > perfection).
- ✅ Check analytics (CTR, watch time, comments) and take notes.

Phase 2: Days 31–60 – Momentum

- ✅ Commit to **2 videos/week** (set calendar).
- ✅ Add engagement boosters: call-to-action + pinned comments.
- ✅ Reply to every viewer comment.
- ✅ A/B test thumbnails & titles → aim for higher CTR.
- ✅ Share videos in 3+ communities & collaborate with a micro-creator.
- ✅ Upload first Shorts for discoverability.

Phase 3: Days 61–90 – Explosion

- ✅ Identify top 3 winning videos → make sequels/spin-offs.
- ✅ Repurpose videos into Shorts.
- ✅ Build 3+ playlists with strong titles.
- ✅ Add end screens + playlist links for binge factor.
- ✅ Reach out to 5 creators → secure 1 collab or podcast guest spot.
- ✅ Enable monetization (ads/affiliates/digital products).

Golden Codes

1. **Hook fast + keep retention high = algorithm boost.**
2. **Consistency beats luck—upload on schedule.**
3. **Engagement is fuel—spark comments, replies, and shares.**
4. **Double down on what works—don't chase random trends.**
5. **Serve first, monetize second—value attracts money.**

Print this page. Tick each action weekly. By Day 90, you'll have:

- A fully optimized channel
- 12–15 videos published
- Playlists + collabs in place
- Monetization ready
- Momentum toward your first 1,000... and beyond

Appendix: The 90-Day YouTube Growth Cheat Sheet

Your quick-reference roadmap to go from zero to unstoppable.

Phase 1: Days 1-30 - Foundation

- ✅ Optimize channel (logo, banner, About, mission statement).
- ✅ Research top 10 channels in your niche.
- ✅ Create 50+ video ideas (Evergreen + Trending + Personal).
- ✅ Upload first 4–6 videos (clarity > perfection).
- ✅ Track analytics (CTR, watch time, comments).

Phase 2: Days 31-60 - Momentum

- ✅ Commit to **2 videos/week** (calendar locked).
- ✅ Add engagement boosters (CTAs + pinned comments).
- ✅ Reply to every comment.
- ✅ A/B test thumbnails + titles.
- ✅ Share in 3+ communities & collab with a micro-creator.
- ✅ Upload Shorts for discoverability.

Phase 3: Days 61-90 - Explosion

- ✅ Identify top 3 winning videos → create sequels.
- ✅ Repurpose videos into Shorts.
- ✅ Build 3+ binge-worthy playlists.
- ✅ Add end screens + playlist links.
- ✅ Reach out to 5 creators → secure 1 collab/guest spot.
- ✅ Enable monetization (ads, affiliates, products).

Golden Codes for Fast Growth

1. Hook fast + retain viewers = algorithm boost.
2. Consistency > luck.
3. Engagement is fuel (comments, replies, shares).
4. Double down on what works.
5. Serve first, monetize second.

Action Tip: Print this page, stick it on your wall, and check off tasks weekly. By Day 90, your channel will have momentum, systems, and a clear growth path toward your first million.

YouTube Earnings in India — How Much Per View?

CPM vs RPM: What's the Difference?

- **CPM (Cost Per Mille)** is what advertisers pay for 1,000 ad impressions.
- **RPM (Revenue Per Mille)** is what creators **actually receive** per 1,000 views *after YouTube's 45% cut* and accounting for monetized views only.
- YouTube takes a 45% commission, so creators receive about 55% of CPM. Wikipedia

Typical Earnings Ranges in India

- **RPM (Actual Earnings per 1,000 Views):** ₹20–₹200 depending on niche, audience, ad formats, and engagement upGradGrowth Rich Hindi Mumbaikarsperspective
- Examples:
- **₹20 per 1,000 views:** Lower-engagement niches like general entertainment, vlogging Growth Rich HindiBoss Wallah Blog
- **₹40–₹80 per 1,000 views:** Moderate-performing channels—lifestyle, mid-tier content Growth Rich HindiFinance Keeda
- **₹80–₹100 (or more):** High-value niches like tech, finance, business Finance KeedaGrowth Rich HindiupGrad

What This Means in Real Numbers

Views Estimated Earnings (₹) Rough USD Equivalent

1,000 ₹20–₹200 ~$0.25–$2.50
10,000 ₹200–₹2,000 ~$2.50–$25
100,000 ₹2,000–₹20,000 ~$25–$250
1,000,000 ₹20,000–₹200,000. ~$250–$2,500

(Broad estimates—actual earnings can vary widely.)

Real-World Examples from Indian Creators

- One creator with 1.4 million views earned just about USD $200 total—highlighting low RPM despite high viewership Reddit.
- Content centered around Indian audiences or general niches often sees lower RPM compared to Western audiences or premium niches. Reddit+2Reddit+2

What Really Affects Earnings

Niche & Audience

- Finance, tech, and business garner higher ad rates. Finance KeedaGrowth Rich Hindi

Geography of Viewers

- Advertisers pay more for viewers in the US, UK, etc. Indian audiences typically yield lower RPM. Reddit+1

Ad Formats & Engagement

- Longer videos (8+ minutes) allow multiple ads. High engagement retains viewers and improves ad efficiency. Growth Rich HindiBoss Wallah Blog

Seasonality

- During festive seasons, ad spends rise—boosting RPM. It often dips in quieter months. Reddit

What Authors/Creators Should Know

- Earnings are not fixed: they're driven by niche, location, ad type, and viewer behavior.
- Expect lower RPM in India compared to Western markets, unless your content appeals globally. Reddit+1
- Even in India, high-performing niches (finance, business) can earn significantly better than average. Finance Keeda

Quick Summary Table

Factor	Typical Range in India
RPM per 1,000 views	₹20 – ₹200
Higher RPM Niches	Tech, Finance, Business
Lower RPM Niches	Vlogging, Entertainment
Estimated Earnings (1M views)	₹20,000 – ₹200,000

Bottom Line:

In India, expected earnings hover between **₹20 and ₹200 per 1,000 views**, translating to **₹20,000–₹200,000 per million views**—depending on your niche and viewer demographics. To maximize revenue, focus on high-value niches, global audiences, longer videos, and engagement.

Estimated YouTube Earnings in India by Niche & Views

1. Entertainment / Vlogging (Low RPM: ₹20–₹50 per 1,000 views)

- 100,000 views → ₹2,000 – ₹5,000
- 500,000 views → ₹10,000 – ₹25,000
- 1,000,000 views → ₹20,000 – ₹50,000

2. Education / Motivation / Tutorials (Mid RPM: ₹50–₹100 per 1,000 views)

- 100,000 views → ₹5,000 – ₹10,000
- 500,000 views → ₹25,000 – ₹50,000
- 1,000,000 views → ₹50,000 – ₹100,000

3. Tech Reviews / Gadgets / Software (Higher RPM: ₹80–₹120 per 1,000 views)

- 100,000 views → ₹8,000 – ₹12,000
- 500,000 views → ₹40,000 – ₹60,000
- 1,000,000 views → ₹80,000 – ₹120,000

4. Finance / Business / Investment (Premium RPM: ₹120–₹200 per 1,000 views)

- 100,000 views → ₹12,000 – ₹20,000
- 500,000 views → ₹60,000 – ₹100,000
- 1,000,000 views → ₹120,000 – ₹200,000

Key Takeaways

- Same view count = **different income** depending on niche.
- Finance/Tech **pay 5–10x more** than Entertainment.
- Longer videos (8+ mins) with multiple ads can boost revenue further.
- If your audience includes **USA/UK viewers**, RPM could be **2–5x higher** than India-only audiences.

Top Niches for YouTube Success (2025)

1. Finance & Money

- Topics: Investing, personal finance, business tips, passive income, side hustles.
- RPM: **₹120–₹200+ per 1,000 views** (highest paying niche).
- Why: Advertisers pay premium for financial audiences; content is evergreen.
- Example: "How to Save ₹1 Lakh in a Year" or "5 Passive Income Ideas in India."

2. Tech & Gadgets

- Topics: Smartphone reviews, software tutorials, AI tools, tech comparisons.
- RPM: **₹80–₹120 per 1,000 views.**
- Why: High search demand, huge affiliate income potential (Amazon, software).
- Example: "Top 5 AI Tools to Save Time in 2025" or "iPhone 15 vs Samsung S25 Review."

3. Education & Career

- Topics: Exam prep, coding tutorials, language learning, skill-building.
- RPM: **₹50–₹100 per 1,000 views.**
- Why: Students & professionals are always searching; content is long-term.
- Example: "Python Tutorial for Beginners" or "How to Crack UPSC in First Attempt."

4. Health, Fitness & Lifestyle

- Topics: Home workouts, diet plans, mental health, productivity hacks.
- RPM: **₹40–₹80 per 1,000 views.**
- Why: Massive demand, loyal audiences, brand sponsorship potential.
- Example: "10 Minute Morning Workout" or "7 Foods That Boost Energy."

5. Motivation & Self-Improvement

- Topics: Success habits, productivity, inspirational stories.
- RPM: **₹50–₹100 per 1,000 views.**
- Why: Easy to create faceless videos (voiceover + stock footage); viral potential.
- Example: "5 Habits That Changed My Life" or "The Secret of Millionaires."

6. Gaming & Esports

- Topics: Gameplays, live streams, reviews, esports commentary.
- RPM: **₹20–₹50 per 1,000 views.**
- Why: Lower RPM, but huge demand + sponsorship/merch potential.
- Example: "Top 10 Tips for BGMI Players" or "GTA VI Gameplay Walkthrough."

7. Food & Cooking

- Topics: Recipes, street food vlogs, kitchen hacks.
- RPM: **₹30–₹70 per 1,000 views.**
- Why: Evergreen + mass appeal. Can combine with affiliate links (cookware, spices).
- Example: "Quick 10-Minute Dinner Recipe" or "Best Street Food in Delhi."

8. Digital Marketing & Online Growth

- Topics: YouTube growth, freelancing, social media marketing, AI tools.
- RPM: **₹70–₹120 per 1,000 views.**
- Why: Exploding demand in India + globally, high affiliate potential.
- Example: "How to Grow on YouTube in 2025" or "Best Freelancing Sites for Beginners."

Pro Tips for Choosing YOUR Niche

1. Pick something you can talk about **consistently for 1–2 years**.
2. Blend **passion + profit** (don't only chase money, but don't ignore it either).
3. If unsure → start with **Education/Skill + Tech/Finance crossover** (e.g., "Digital Skills for Students").

Always check search demand (Google Trends + YouTube search).

21

Tips Before Applying for YouTube AdSense

1. Meet the Monetization Eligibility

- At least **1,000 subscribers**.
- At least **4,000 watch hours in the past 12 months** OR **10 million Shorts views in the last 90 days**.
- No active **community guideline strikes**.

2. Professional Channel Setup

- Clear **channel name** (avoid copyright issues).
- Attractive **logo + banner** (professional branding).
- Complete **About section** with keywords & description.
- Organized **playlists** and content categories.

3. Upload Original Content Only

- Don't use **copyrighted music, clips, or TV footage**.
- Even if "fair use" is claimed, YouTube is very strict.
- Use royalty-free music (Epidemic Sound, YouTube Audio Library).

4. Build Consistency First

- Upload at least **15–20 quality videos** before applying.
- This shows YouTube your channel is **serious and active**.
- Consistent posting = stronger algorithm trust.

5. Verify Your Channel

- Add a **phone number verification**.
- Enable **2-step verification** on your Google account (mandatory for monetization).

6. Check Your Niche

- Some niches have stricter rules (kids content, reused content, "made-for-kids" channels).
- Clearly mark your audience settings (general vs. kids).

7. Content Quality & Engagement

- Thumbnails + Titles should be professional.
- At least 2–3 minutes average watch time per video.
- Encourage likes, comments, and shares.

8. Location & Bank Setup

- Use your **real name, address, and bank details** (no fake info).
- Make sure your **PAN card** and **bank account** are ready (for India).
- AdSense will send a **PIN by post** to verify your address.

9. Avoid Policy Violations

- No misleading thumbnails/titles ("clickbait scams").
- No hate speech, adult content, or shocking violence.
- Read **YouTube Partner Program policies** carefully.

10. Be Patient

- After applying, AdSense review can take **a few days to a few weeks**.
- If rejected, you can reapply after 30 days (fix issues before reapplying).

22

Ways to Earn Money from YouTube Without Monetization

1. Affiliate Marketing

- Promote products/services in your videos and put affiliate links in the description.
- Example: Tech channel → Amazon affiliate links for phones, laptops.
- Example: Fitness channel → Protein supplements or workout gear.
- Income: ₹500 – ₹5,000+ per sale depending on product.

2. Sponsorships & Brand Deals

- Even small channels (5K–10K subs) can get **micro-sponsorships**.
- Reach out to brands in your niche → offer product reviews or shoutouts.
- Example: A cooking channel can get kitchenware sponsorships.
- Income: ₹2,000 – ₹50,000 per video (depends on niche & reach).

3. Selling Your Own Digital Products

- Ebooks, courses, templates, cheat sheets, music, stock footage.
- Example: "YouTube Growth Guide PDF" or "Online Course on Video

Editing."

- Platforms: Gumroad, Teachable, Thinkific.
- Income: Unlimited (one-time effort → long-term passive sales).

4. Merchandise (T-Shirts, Mugs, Hoodies, etc.)

- Print-on-demand (no inventory needed).
- Use platforms like **TeeSpring, Printify, Redbubble**.
- Example: Gaming channel → funny gaming quotes on T-shirts.
- Income: ₹200 – ₹500 per item sold.

5. Crowdfunding & Donations

- Ask your loyal audience to support via **Patreon, BuyMeACoffee, PayPal**.
- Offer perks: exclusive videos, behind-the-scenes, Q&A access.
- Example: Motivational channel → "Support my mission for daily motivation."
- Income: Recurring monthly support.

6. Freelancing / Services via YouTube

- Use your channel to **showcase skills** → attract clients.
- Example: Video editor shows tutorials → gets editing projects.
- Example: Marketing expert shares tips → lands consulting clients.
- Income: ₹5,000 – ₹1,00,000+ per client depending on service.

7. Lead Generation for Your Business

- YouTube = free traffic source.
- Example: Fitness trainer posts free workouts → sells paid personal coaching.
- Example: Agency posts case studies → lands new business deals.
- Income: Directly tied to value of clients/customers.

8. YouTube Shorts Fund (Old) → Now "Creator Rewards"

- YouTube sometimes pays creators for viral Shorts (₹10,000+ rewards).
- Not AdSense—special creator programs run by YouTube.

9. Sell Stock Footage or Music

- Create cinematic clips, b-roll, or background music.
- Sell them on **Storyblocks, Pond5, Shutterstock, Artlist**.
- Your channel becomes a funnel to your stock library.

10. Consulting & Coaching

- Once you build authority, people will **pay for your guidance**.
- Example: Small YouTuber helping others start channels.
- Example: Language tutor offering private classes.
- Income: ₹500 – ₹10,000 per session.

Golden Rule:

Ads are the *smallest* income source for many creators. The **real money** is in **affiliates, products, sponsorships, and services.**

23

How to Earn Money on YouTube Without Monetization

When people think of YouTube earnings, they only imagine those little yellow dollar signs from AdSense. But here's the truth: **ads are not the only way to earn money**. In fact, some of the biggest creators earn more from outside opportunities than from YouTube's ad program.

And the best part? You don't need to wait until you hit 1,000 subscribers or 4,000 watch hours. You can start earning **from Day One** if you play smart.

1. Affiliate Marketing – Earn While You Sleep

Affiliate marketing is one of the fastest ways to start making money. All you do is promote a product you genuinely recommend and place a special link in your video description. When someone buys through your link, you earn a commission.

- Example: A tech channel can share Amazon affiliate links to phones, laptops, or headphones.
- Example: A fitness channel can promote protein powders, supplements,

or gym equipment.
- Earnings Potential: ₹500 – ₹5,000+ per sale depending on product.

Pro Tip: Always be honest. Only promote products you trust, or you'll lose your audience's respect.

2. Sponsorships & Brand Deals - Even with Small Channels

You don't need millions of subscribers to land a brand deal. Many companies look for **micro-influencers** (small but loyal audiences).

- Example: A cooking channel gets free kitchenware + ₹10,000 per sponsored video.
- Example: A lifestyle channel reviews skincare products and earns brand sponsorships.
- Earnings Potential: ₹2,000 – ₹50,000 per video depending on audience size.

Pro Tip: Don't wait for brands to find you—send them a professional email introducing your channel and offering collaboration.

3. Selling Your Own Digital Products

Why just promote other people's products when you can sell your own? Digital products have zero cost to reproduce and can sell forever.

Ideas:

- Ebooks ("30 Recipes Under 15 Minutes")
- Online courses ("YouTube Growth for Beginners")
- Templates, presets, checklists, or guides.

Pro Tip: Use platforms like Gumroad or Teachable. Upload once, and let YouTube drive sales forever.

4. Freelancing & Services Through YouTube

Your YouTube channel can be the best portfolio you'll ever create. Show your skills, and people will pay you for them.

- Example: A video editor shares tutorials → lands editing clients.
- Example: A digital marketer shares strategies → gets consulting projects.

Earnings Potential: ₹5,000 – ₹1,00,000+ per client depending on your skill.

5. Merchandising - Turn Fans into Walking Billboards

If you have a strong brand or catchphrases, consider selling merchandise. Print-on-demand platforms handle everything from printing to shipping.
Ideas:

- T-shirts with your slogan.
- Mugs with funny quotes.
- Hoodies with your channel logo.

Pro Tip: Don't launch merch too early. Wait until you have at least 5,000–10,000 loyal fans.

6. Donations & Crowdfunding

Platforms like **Patreon, BuyMeACoffee, or PayPal** allow fans to directly support your channel.

- Example: A motivational channel offers exclusive behind-the-scenes content for ₹200/month support.
- Example: A music channel lets fans request custom covers in exchange for donations.

7. Coaching & Consulting

Once you establish authority, people will pay to learn directly from you.

- Example: A fitness creator offers personal coaching calls.
- Example: A YouTube strategist sells one-on-one consulting sessions.

8. Lead Generation for Your Business

If you already run a business, YouTube can act as your free lead magnet.

- A lawyer making legal advice videos → attracts new clients.
- A designer showing tutorials → gets freelance projects.

Golden Truth: Monetization Is Just the Beginning

Ads are great, but they're often the **smallest income source** for creators. If you focus only on AdSense, you're limiting yourself. The **real wealth** comes from affiliates, products, sponsorships, and services.

Action Steps for You

- Pick **one method** from above and implement it this week.
- Add your affiliate link, product link, or service offer in your video description.
- Remind your viewers in the video to "Check the link below."
- Track results and scale what works.

Remember: You don't need YouTube to approve you to start earning. You only need an idea, a little creativity, and the courage to put yourself out there.

If you treat your channel like a business from Day One, the money will follow—even before the ads start rolling.

24

Real-Life Examples of Indian Creators Earning Beyond AdSense

1. Technical Guruji (Gaurav Chaudhary) – Tech Reviews

- One of India's biggest tech YouTubers.
- Majority of his revenue doesn't come from YouTube ads, but from **brand deals, product sponsorships, and affiliate sales**.
- Example: Every phone review links to Amazon/Flipkart affiliate programs. With millions of views, that means crores in affiliate earnings.

2. Ranveer Allahbadia (BeerBiceps) – Self-Improvement & Business

- Started with fitness, now covers entrepreneurship, motivation, podcasts.
- Income streams: **brand partnerships, his startup (Monk Entertainment), and courses**.
- He openly shares that **YouTube ads are just a small part** of his income. His real money comes from **businesses built on top of YouTube visibility**.

3. Neha Sharma (Cook with Nisha) – Food Niche

- She monetized through **recipe ebooks, cooking workshops, and kitchen**

product sponsorships.

- Even before massive views, she used affiliate links for cookware and spices, which her audience bought regularly.

4. Digital Deepak (Deepak Kanakaraju) – Digital Marketing

- Built his YouTube channel as a **lead-generation machine**.
- Offers paid online courses, workshops, and freelancing services.
- Uses free YouTube content to build trust → converts viewers into **paying students**.

5. Sahil Khan (Fitness Influencer) – Health & Fitness

- His real income comes from **fitness supplements, gym franchise, and brand promotions**, not ads.
- He uses YouTube to **market his brand empire**, proving creators can earn crores without depending on AdSense.

Key Lesson from These Creators

- They **don't wait** for AdSense.
- They treat YouTube as a **business funnel**, not just a video platform.
- They use YouTube to:
- Build authority.
- Gain audience trust.
- Sell products/services.
- Land sponsorships.

Takeaway for Readers:

If India's biggest creators rely more on affiliates, sponsors, and their own products than on ads—**you should too**. AdSense is just a bonus, not the main game.

Mini-Chapter: Proof – How Top Indian Creators Earn Beyond Ads

Most new YouTubers believe that once their channel is monetized, they'll start earning lakhs every month. But here's the secret: **AdSense is just the bonus money.** The real wealth comes from sponsors, affiliates, products, and services.

Let's look at how some of India's most successful creators make money **outside AdSense**:

1. Technical Guruji (Gaurav Chaudhary) – Tech Reviews

- Millions of views on every phone review.
- But ads aren't his main source of income.
- His real earnings come from **Amazon/Flipkart affiliate sales** and **brand sponsorships**.
- Every review video description is packed with affiliate links → lakhs in passive income.

2. Ranveer Allahbadia (BeerBiceps) – Self-Improvement & Business

- Built his name on fitness, then expanded into business, podcasts, and motivation.
- Runs **Monk Entertainment**, his media company.
- Earnings come from **brand deals, online courses, and his businesses**.
- YouTube ads? Just pocket money compared to his larger ventures.

3. Cook with Nisha (Neha Sharma) – Food Niche

- A small-to-medium creator compared to giants, but a great example.
- Earns through **ebooks, recipe courses, and cookware sponsorships**.
- Even with fewer views, her affiliate links bring in regular income from

kitchen products.

4. Digital Deepak (Deepak Kanakaraju) - Marketing Education

- Uses YouTube as a **lead generator**.
- Posts free content to build trust.
- Then converts viewers into **paid students for his courses and workshops**.
- Proves YouTube is not just about ads—it's about **building a business funnel**.

5. Sahil Khan - Fitness & Lifestyle

- Former Bollywood actor turned fitness influencer.
- Runs a supplement brand and a gym franchise business.
- Uses YouTube mainly as a **marketing platform** for his products.
- Earnings: Crores from business ventures, not YouTube ads.

Lessons from These Creators

- None of them depend only on AdSense.
- They use YouTube to **build trust → grow an audience → sell products/services.**
- Whether you're a beginner or advanced creator, your mindset should be:

"YouTube is my stage. The real money is in the business I build around it."

This mini-chapter gives your readers **confidence**: they'll see proof that big names don't rely on ads alone, so they shouldn't either.

Mini-Chapter: How Much Do Top Indian YouTubers Earn Monthly?

One of the biggest motivators for new creators is knowing the *real numbers.* How much do successful YouTubers actually earn every month? While exact figures are private, industry reports, sponsorship rates, and analytics tools give us solid estimates.

Here's a breakdown of **top Indian creators and their approximate monthly earnings**:

1. Ranveer Allahbadia (BeerBiceps) - Self-Improvement & Business

- **YouTube Ads + Content**: ₹8–10 lakh/month
- **Brand Collaborations & Sponsorships**: ₹15–20 lakh/month
- **Podcast (The Ranveer Show)**: ₹5–7 lakh/month
- **Online Courses & Businesses**: ₹5–10 lakh/month
- **Total Estimated Monthly Earnings: ~₹35 lakh+**

Lesson: Ranveer proves that diversifying income streams is the real secret to wealth.

2. Technical Guruji (Gaurav Chaudhary) - Tech Reviews

- **YouTube Ads Alone**: USD 6,600–9,100/month (₹5.4–7.4 lakh)
- **Brand Sponsorships & Affiliate Links**: Easily 2x–3x the ad income
- **Total Estimated Monthly Earnings: ₹15–20 lakh+**

Lesson: Tech channels are gold mines for affiliate sales and brand deals.

3. Nisha Madhulika – Cooking & Recipes

- **YouTube Ads**: ₹2–4 lakh/month
- **Cookware Sponsorships & Brand Deals**: ₹3–5 lakh/month
- **Books, Events, & Recipe Products**: ₹1–2 lakh/month
- **Total Estimated Monthly Earnings: ₹6–10 lakh**

Lesson: Even a niche like cooking can be highly profitable with the right partnerships.

4. Digital Deepak (Deepak Kanakaraju) – Digital Marketing Education

- **YouTube Ads**: ₹1–2 lakh/month
- **Courses & Workshops**: ₹10–15 lakh/month
- **Consulting & Freelancing Projects**: ₹5–8 lakh/month
- **Total Estimated Monthly Earnings: ₹18–25 lakh**

Lesson: YouTube as a funnel for high-value services beats ad revenue every time.

5. Sahil Khan – Fitness & Lifestyle

- **YouTube Ads**: ₹2–3 lakh/month
- **Fitness Supplements & Merch**: ₹10–15 lakh/month
- **Gym Franchise & Business Deals**: ₹20–25 lakh/month
- **Total Estimated Monthly Earnings: ₹30–40 lakh**

Lesson: Build a brand empire beyond YouTube, and the earnings multiply.

Final Takeaway for Readers

These earnings prove that YouTube is not just about **uploading videos for ads**. It's about **leveraging attention, building trust, and turning your influence into multiple income streams**.

If India's biggest creators rely more on affiliates, sponsorships, and products than AdSense, **you should too**.

Mini Income Blueprint: How to Earn Like the Pros in Your Niche

Not every creator has the same path. A cooking channel, a tech reviewer, and a motivational speaker can't all use the same income strategy. That's why it's important to tailor your earning model to your niche.

Here's a simple breakdown inspired by India's top creators:

🔷 *If You're in Tech (like Technical Guruji)*

- **Affiliate Marketing**: Add Amazon/Flipkart links for every gadget.
- **Sponsorships**: Partner with smartphone brands, app companies, or gadget makers.
- **Courses/Workshops**: Teach "How to start a tech channel" or "How to buy the right phone."
- *Income Potential*: ₹10–20 lakh/month once you have 100K+ loyal followers.

🔹 *If You're in Cooking/Food (like Nisha Madhulika)*

- **Affiliate Links**: Cookware, appliances, spices.
- **Ebooks**: "100 Quick Recipes for Beginners."
- **Workshops**: Paid live cooking classes or online recipe lessons.
- **Brand Deals**: Collaborations with food & kitchen brands.
- *Income Potential*: ₹5–10 lakh/month with 50K–100K strong subscribers.

🔹 *If You're in Education/Marketing (like Digital Deepak)*

- **Courses**: Create structured video lessons.
- **Workshops & Webinars**: Live training for ₹499–₹999 per student.
- **Consulting**: High-ticket services for businesses/individuals.
- **Books & PDFs**: Sell guides on Amazon or Gumroad.
- *Income Potential*: ₹15–25 lakh/month with 30K–50K targeted subscribers.

🔹 *If You're in Fitness/Lifestyle (like Sahil Khan)*

- **Supplements**: Launch your own brand or partner with existing ones.
- **Merchandise**: Fitness T-shirts, bottles, accessories.
- **Coaching**: Paid 1:1 or group workout programs.
- **Franchises/Events**: Gym franchises or health events.
- *Income Potential*: ₹20–40 lakh/month with 100K–200K engaged subscribers.

🔹 *If You're in Motivation/Personal Growth (like BeerBiceps)*

- **Brand Deals**: Self-growth apps, book launches, finance tools.
- **Podcast Sponsorships**: Invite guests and charge brands for slots.
- **Courses/Books**: Build a library of personal development products.
- **Community Memberships**: Exclusive clubs or masterminds.
- *Income Potential*: ₹20–35 lakh/month with a loyal base of 100K–200K subs.

Your Action Plan

1. Identify your niche.
2. Pick **2–3 monetization models** from above (don't try everything at once).
3. Add at least **one monetization link or offer** in your next upload.
4. Scale as your channel grows.

Golden Rule: Don't wait for monetization. If you have even 500–1000 subscribers, you can start testing affiliates, ebooks, or small workshops right now.

Mini Income Blueprint: How to Earn Like the Pros

Tech (like Technical Guruji)

- Affiliate links (Amazon, Flipkart)
- Sponsorships with gadget brands
- Paid tech workshops

₹10–20 lakh

Cooking/Food (like Nisha Madhulika)

- Cookware & appliance affiliates
- Recipe ebooks
- Paid online classes
- Brand collaborations

₹5–10 lakh

Education/Marketing (like Digital Deepak)

- Online courses
- Webinars/workshops
- Consulting & freelancing

- Books/PDFs

₹15–25 lakh

Fitness/Lifestyle (like Sahil Khan)

- Supplements & nutrition
- Merchandise (T-shirts, bottles)
- Coaching programs
- Franchises/events

₹20–40 lakh

Motivation/Personal Growth (like BeerBiceps)

- Brand deals & sponsorships
- Podcast monetization
- Courses & books
- Exclusive memberships

₹20–35 lakh

Quick Action Steps

1. Pick your niche.
2. Select **2–3 income streams** to start with.
3. Add them in your video descriptions immediately.
4. Scale up as your subscribers grow.

This table instantly shows your readers: *"If my niche is X, here's how I can earn money like the pros."*

YouTube Income Blueprint – Cheat Sheet

Step 1: Choose Your Niche

- Tech
- Cooking/Food
- Education/Marketing
- Fitness/Lifestyle
- Motivation/Personal Growth

Step 2: Monetization Roadmap by Niche

Niche
Top 3–4 Income Streams
Earning Potential (Monthly)

Tech
Affiliate links (Amazon/Flipkart), Brand Sponsorships, Paid Workshops
₹10–20 lakh
Cooking/Food
Cookware & Appliance Affiliates, Recipe Ebooks, Online Classes, Brand Deals
₹5–10 lakh
Education/Marketing
Online Courses, Webinars, Consulting, Books/PDFs
₹15–25 lakh
Fitness/Lifestyle
Supplements, Merchandise, Coaching, Events/Franchises
₹20–40 lakh
Motivation/Personal Growth
Brand Sponsorships, Podcasts, Courses/Books, Memberships
₹20–35 lakh

Step 3: Quick Action Plan
✅ Pick **2–3 monetization streams** in your niche.

✅ Add links/offers in your next upload (don't wait for AdSense).
✅ Build trust → Promote valuable products → Scale income.

Golden Rule: YouTube is not the income. YouTube is the stage.
The real money comes from the **business around your channel.**

90-Day YouTube Income Blueprint – Cheat Sheet

Phase 1: Day 1–30 → Build Trust & Audience Foundation

Goal: Establish credibility & plant seeds for monetization.

- Upload 8–12 valuable videos (focus on solving problems/entertaining).
- Optimize titles, thumbnails & descriptions (SEO friendly).
- Start adding **soft CTAs** ("Link in description" without heavy selling).
- Research affiliate programs in your niche (Amazon, Flipkart, brand sites).
- Collect viewer emails with a free giveaway (recipe PDF, cheat sheet, eBook, etc.).

Phase 2: Day 31–60 → Add Affiliates & Light Monetization

Goal: Start earning your first income even with small audience.

- Add **affiliate links** in every new and old video.
- Create your first **small digital product** (recipe eBook, mini-course, checklist).
- Reach out for **micro-sponsorships** (brands often pay even for 5K–10K subs if your niche is right).
- Start doing **live streams/webinars** to connect deeply with your audience.
- Track analytics: double down on videos with highest watch time & CTR.

Phase 3: Day 61–90 → Launch Products & Scale

Goal: Move from side-income to serious creator business.

- Launch your **first paid product/service**:
- Tech → Paid workshop/webinar.
- Cooking → Premium recipe eBook or cooking class.
- Education → Course/masterclass.
- Fitness → Coaching package.
- Motivation → Membership group.
- Collaborate with other creators in your niche to tap into new audiences.
- Negotiate **sponsorship deals** with at least 2–3 brands.
- Build a **simple sales funnel** (YouTube → Email → Paid Offer).
- Analyze income sources → Scale the one with highest ROI.

Your 90-Day Income Milestones

- **Day 1–30:** 0 → 1,000 subscribers, email list started, affiliate programs ready.
- **Day 31–60:** First affiliate commission + small digital product launched.
- **Day 61–90:** First ₹10,000–₹50,000 earned (depending on niche & effort), brand deals begin.

Golden Rule: Don't wait for monetization. Treat your YouTube like a **business from Day 1**—products, affiliates, and partnerships bring income far earlier than AdSense.

This cheat sheet works like a **bridge** between your *90-Day Growth Blueprint* and *Income Blueprint*. It ensures readers grow **subscribers + income** side by side.

25

Invitations to Join My Community

Congratulations! You now have the roadmap to **shift your mindset and start building wealth**. If you're ready to **accelerate your journey**, I've created a complete online course. You can also connect with me on social media to get updates, free resources, and ongoing mentorship. Just search for **"Tarun Takshay"** and join the community. Your Digital Empire Awaits. Transform Your Life, Mindset, and Business.

Are you ready to break free from limitations, unlock wealth, and build a business that works for you 24/7? In Digital Empire, Tarun Takshay shares the proven strategies, systems, and mindset shifts that turn dreamers into digital CEOs. Inside this book, you'll discover:

- How to think and act like a millionaire even if you're starting from zero
- Step-by-step frameworks to build scalable digital businesses
- Actionable templates, checklists, and tools to turn ideas into income
- A roadmap to create freedom, impact, and legacy
- Provides step-by-step guidance to start and scale your side hustle.
- Shares templates, worksheets, and action plans for beginners.
- Offers a community of like-minded learners for support and accountability.
- Includes case studies and strategies to fast-track your first ₹10k, ₹50k,

and beyond.

Take the next step:

"Ready to take the next step? Explore my online courses, join live webinars, and access exclusive templates and blueprints to accelerate your journey from knowledge to real digital income. Visit www.takshaydigitalacademy.com *and start building your digital empire today!"*

Visit to join our courses

Join now and turn your side hustle into **real financial freedom**.

Series Companion Map – "Digital Wealth Ecosystem"

Here's how Book 12 fits into the **full 12-book ecosystem** and funnels you to courses and actionable income:

Step 1 – Mindset & Foundation

- Book 1: Digital Coach Blueprint
- Book 2: 10X Digital Coach Mastery
- Book 3: 10X Funnel Mindset Secrets

Step 2 – Ads, Funnels, and Business Skills

- Book 4: Meta Ads Secrets
- Book 5: Google Ads Secrets
- Book 6: Digital Empire 100 CR Club, A billionaire mindset

Step 3 – Financial Mindset & Side Hustle Growth

- Book 7: Rock Bottom to Digital Freedom

- Book 8: Middle-Class Trap to Millionaire Mindset
- Book 9: Side Hustle to Financial Freedom

Step 4 – AI & Social Media Mastery

- Book 10: Decode YouTube Algorithm
- Book 11: Decode Instagram Algorithm
- Book 12: The AI Millionaire

Step 5 – Courses & Live Coaching

- Use these books as your roadmap to digital freedom
- Each book includes exercises, worksheets, and companion resources
- Join courses and webinars to scale faster and automate income

Let's Stay Connected

The author would like to interact with you and receive your feedback. Get in touch and send him your reviews

www.takshaydigitalacademy.com
www.taruntakshay.com
tarun@taruntakshay.com
www.youtube.com/digitaltakshay
www.instagram.com/taruntakshay
www.facebook.com/taruntakshay
https://www.linkedin.com/in/tarun-takshay/
https://digitaltakshay.com/

📧 You can reach me directly at: **info@takshaydigitalacademy.com**
🌐 Or visit my website: https://www.takshaydigitalacademy.com/

Thank you !

This book may end here, but our journey together doesn't have to. I'd love to hear your story—what resonated with you, what breakthroughs you experienced, and how you're applying these systems in your coaching business.

💎 Part of the Digital Empire Series – Your Complete Transformation Journey:

- Middle Class Trap to Millionaire Mindset
- Digital Coach Blueprint
- 10X Digital Coach Mastery
- Digital Empire Millionaire Mindset: 100 CR Club

🌐 Take your next step now:

Visit www.takshaydigitalacademy.com for exclusive resources, free templates, mini-courses, and advanced strategies to scale your digital business.

Start building your Digital Empire today — the world is waiting for your impact.

About the Author

You can connect with me on:

https://www.takshaydigitalacademy.com

Also by Tarun Takshay

www.ingramcontent.com/pod-product-compliance
Ingram Content Group UK Ltd.
Pitfield, Milton Keynes, MK11 3LW, UK
UKHW021408190726
13845UKWH00028B/954

9 789334 449891